Divine Trinity: Apologetics for the Triune God

M.J. Kelley II

Published by M.J. Kelley II, 2024.

While every precaution has been taken in the preparation of this book, the publisher assumes no responsibility for errors or omissions, or for damages resulting from the use of the information contained herein.

DIVINE TRINITY: APOLOGETICS FOR THE TRIUNE GOD

First edition. May 15, 2024.

Copyright © 2024 M.J. Kelley II.

ISBN: 979-8224826049

Written by M.J. Kelley II.

Table of Contents

I would first like to start off by thanking the Lord of Glory for choosing me. I know me, and there is no way I would have picked myself to write a book about His Holy Character as the Triune God. I am in awe of this incredible opportunity to explore and share His Holy Character with the world. The LORD of lords, the King of kings, the Alpha and the Omega, the First and the Last, the God of Israel.

Studying the Trinity has undoubtedly been a great spiritual blessing for me. The concept of the Triune God, three distinct persons in one divine being, has deepened my understanding and appreciation for the complexity and mystery of divine nature. Through studying the Trinity, I have gained a profound sense of awe and reverence for God's infinite nature and His ability to exist in perfect unity and harmony as Father, Son, and Holy Spirit.

Furthermore, delving into the study of the Trinity has equipped me with a stronger apologetic to defend the Triune Nature of God. In engaging with skeptics and those who question the validity of the Trinity, I am now able to articulate clear and compelling arguments that support this foundational doctrine of Christianity. The knowledge I have acquired through my study has given me confidence in defending the Triune Nature of God, as I am able to explain how the three persons of the Trinity are distinct yet unified in their essence.

Moreover, my study of the Trinity has helped me to better understand and appreciate the role that each person in the Trinity plays in our lives. I have come to recognize the love and grace of God the Father, the redemptive work of Jesus Christ as the Son, and the guidance and empowerment of the Holy Spirit. This understanding has deepened my relationship with God and has allowed me to experience His presence and power in a more profound way.

Studying the Trinity has been a transformative journey for me. It has not only enriched my spiritual life but also equipped me to defend and articulate the Triune Nature of God. The study has deepened my understanding of God's nature and His work in our lives. I am truly grateful for this spiritual blessing and the opportunity to grow in my faith through this exploration of the Trinity. My prayer is that you will get a deeper understanding of the Triune God as you read through this book.

In the journey of bringing a book to life, the collaborative effort of uniquely talented individuals is indispensable. It is with immense gratitude that I extend my heartfelt thanks to David M. Cenicola, M.Ed., whose editorial prowess transformed my initial manuscript into a literary masterpiece. David's keen eye for detail, coupled with his profound understanding of narrative flow and structural coherence, has been instrumental in elevating the quality of the work far beyond my expectations. His dedication and skill have not only polished the text but also ensured that the essence of the narrative was magnified in its clarity and impact.

Equally deserving of praise is Alyssa Scott, whose exceptional talent as an illustrator brought a new dimension of engagement to the book. Alyssa took my rudimentary notes and breathed life into them through her art, creating visual ads that not only complemented but significantly enhanced the points being made throughout the narrative. Her creative vision and ability to translate complex concepts into compelling visuals have added a layer of depth and accessibility to the book, making it more appealing and understandable to the reader.

Special thanks must also be extended to Dr. Fatima Zahra, whose expertise in Electro-Mechanical Engineering and insights into the multidimensional realm provided a unique perspective that enriched the content significantly. Her contributions have allowed us to explore and present the concept of the Triune God in a manner that is both innovative and profound. Dr. Zahra's knowledge and passion for her field have opened up new avenues of thought within the book, offering readers a deeper understanding of the subject matter from an interdisciplinary standpoint.

The synthesis of David's editorial genius, Alyssa's artistic flair, and Dr. Zahra's scientific acumen has been nothing short of miraculous. Together, they have helped to transform my vision into a tangible reality, turning the pages of this book into a journey that I hope will resonate with many. Their collective efforts have not only enhanced the book's quality but have also been a source of inspiration for me personally. I am deeply grateful for their contributions and proud to have worked alongside such extraordinary individuals in this creative endeavor.

As I reflect on the journey of writing this book, my heart swells with immense gratitude towards my beautiful wife, Denisse. For 14 years, she has been my steadfast partner, and her support has never wavered, especially during the long nights spent in the quiet pursuit of this project and others. Denisse's understanding and patience have been a beacon of light, allowing me to delve deep into my work, knowing that it is done for the Glory of the Lord. Her ability to quietly shoulder additional responsibilities while I am engrossed in my writing is a testament to her strength, love, and commitment to our shared values and goals. This book is not just a result of my efforts but a manifestation of Denisse's sacrifice and belief in the purpose behind it. For this, and for so much more, I am eternally grateful. Her unwavering support emboldens me to continue on this path, making our journey together all the more meaningful.

Prayer before starting the book

Heavenly Father, I come before You today with a heart yearning for a deeper comprehension of Your divine character. I recognize that in understanding who You are, I not only draw nearer to You but am also empowered to reflect Your light in this world that so often seems shrouded in darkness. Lord, I acknowledge that Your character is the foundation of all truth, love, and righteousness. Your unchanging nature provides me with a steadfast source of hope and comfort amidst the ever-changing tides of life.

I pray, O God, that You would open the eyes of my heart, allowing me to see You more clearly. May the Holy Spirit work within me, revealing the facets of Your character that remain unknown or misunderstood. Let this revelation not just be an accumulation of knowledge, but let it stir a fire within my soul—a fervent desire to live out Your love and grace in my day-to-day life.

Grant me, Lord, the courage and strength to be a light in the darkness, to stand firm in Your truth while showing compassion and mercy as You do. In understanding Your character more fully, may I become a conduit of Your love, peace, and justice, drawing others towards You through my words and actions.

May this prayer not just echo in my heart but resonate through my life, transforming me into a beacon of Your light. In Jesus' name, I pray. AMEN.

Page

Divine Trinity: Apologetics for the Triune God

Introduction:

In the pages of this book, we embark on a profound journey of biblical exploration, seeking to unravel the complexities and mysteries surrounding the Divine Trinity. As we delve into the scripture, we are confronted with the powerful words of Isaiah 45:18 and 46:9, challenging us to contemplate the essence and attributes of God that set Him apart from all others.

Throughout history, the interchangeable use of names such as God, El, Elohim, YHVH, and Adoni has sparked debate, particularly when applied to Jesus or the Holy Spirit. Yet, as Trinitarians, we simply read the Bible word for word, seeking to understand the profound connections and implications of these Divine titles.

The roots of the Godhead concepts, particularly the presence of a second YHVH figure, can be traced back to the Old Testament. In the New Testament, these ancient conceptions find new relevance as they are applied to Jesus, forming the foundation of Trinitarian theology.

As we navigate the intricate landscape of scripture, it becomes clear that heretical teachings often stem from a failure to "rightly divide the word of God." The entirety of the Bible is written for us, but not always to us, compelling us to approach its teachings with humility and discernment.

Any claim that the Trinity was a creation of an early church council reflects a profound ignorance of the Old Testament, where the foundations of this doctrine are firmly rooted. Jesus emerges as the centerpiece, connecting the Holy Spirit to God the Father and forming the bedrock of trinitarian theology.

We come to understand that God is not only a singular essence but also exists in three distinct Persons: Father, Son, and Holy Spirit. The Deity of Christ, often the target of attack, holds the very essence of saving power, underscoring the importance of defending this fundamental truth.

As we meticulously trace the use of YHVH in the Old Testament and its application to Jesus in the New Testament, we are led to the profound conclusion that Jesus is indeed God, *and one with God.* It is my prayer that through this apologetic exegetical study, you too will come to embrace the truth of the One True God of Israel.

Verbiage to Know

Old Testament Verbiage

In the vast and complex world of the Old Testament, it is important for readers to have a solid understanding of certain key terms and definitions. These definitions not only provide clarity and context but also serve as pillars upon which the entire narrative is built. Among these definitions are the terms LORD, Lord, YHVH, GOD, God, and god. Each term carries a distinct meaning and significance within the biblical text, and grasping these meanings will enhance our understanding of the Old Testament as a whole.

Firstly, we encounter the term "LORD" in the Old Testament, often written in capital letters. This term refers to the Divine name of God, known as Yahweh, Jehovah, YHVH, or YHWH. It is a sacred and holy name reserved for the one true God. The LORD represents God's personal and intimate relationship with His chosen people, Israel. It signifies His covenantal faithfulness, His sovereignty, and His supreme authority over all creation.

On the other hand, we also encounter the term "Lord" in the Old Testament, written with an uppercase "L" and lowercase "ord." This term addresses a person of authority or someone who is higher in rank than oneself. In some instances, it can be used to refer to God but without invoking the Divine name. The term "Lord" is often applied to humans, such as kings or rulers, to denote their position of power and authority.

Furthermore, we encounter the term "YHVH," which is the Hebrew name for God. It is often represented by four consonants (YHWH) known as the Tetragrammaton and can be used interchangeably with "Yahweh." Due to its sacredness, this name was considered too holy to be spoken aloud and was replaced with the term "Adonai" (meaning "Lord") when reading aloud from the Hebrew scriptures. YHVH represents God's eternal nature, emphasizing His unchanging character and everlasting presence.

Additionally, the term "GOD" in uppercase letters is often used as a translation for the Hebrew word "Elohim." It is a generic term that often refers to a deity or god in a more general sense, but it is also used in some translations from the original Hebrew to Greek when referring to the one true God of Israel. When referring to the one true God of Israel, however, it carries a more specific meaning and conveys His power, authority, and Divinity.

The term "god" in lowercase letters is used to refer to deities or gods that are worshipped by other nations or cultures. When used in the context of the Old Testament, it frequently refers to false gods or idols that people who have turned away from the one true God worship.

Lastly, we encounter the term "God" with an uppercase "G" in various instances throughout the Old Testament. This term is used interchangeably with LORD and YHVH to refer to the one true God of Israel. It signifies His uniqueness, His greatness, and His position as the ultimate authority over all creation.

Understanding these definitions and distinctions is essential for comprehending the rich tapestry of theological concepts presented in the Old Testament. They provide us with a framework through which we can explore themes of covenant, redemption, worship, and Divine intervention. By delving into these definitions, readers can better appreciate the profound messages conveyed in this ancient collection of texts.

New Testament Verbiage

These Old Testament Divine names, LORD, Lord, YHVH, GOD, god, and God, hold significant meaning and convey different aspects of the Divine nature as well as other entities. However, these Divine names are rendered differently when translating the Old Testament from Hebrew to Greek. It is when we look into the translations that we learn a great deal about God's Word. The Divine name LORD is translated as Χριστός (Messiah) or κύριος (Lord), Lord is translated as κύριος (Lord), and God or god is translated as θεός (God or god). This translation process raises intriguing questions about the nuances and implications of these different renderings.

The choice to translate the Divine name LORD as Χριστός (Messiah) in Greek adds a layer of complexity to our understanding of the Divine nature. The term Χριστός carries a rich historical and theological context, referring to the anointed one or the chosen one. By translating LORD as Χριστός, we are presented with a deeper understanding of God's role as the one who is anointed and chosen to fulfill His Divine plan. It becomes clear that in the transition from the Old Testament to the New Testament the Divine name LORD translates to God as Jesus and that He is clearly the anointed one.

In the New Testament, the translation of "Lord" or "LORD" when it is used to refer to God as "κυριος" in Greek adds depth to our exploration of the Divine nature. κυριος carries connotations of authority, mastery, and sovereignty. By translating Lord as κυριος, we are reminded of God's supreme authority and His role as the ruler and master of all creation. This translation highlights the Divine attributes of power and control, prompting us to reflect on our own relationship with God as our ultimate authority.

The translation of God or god as θεός in Greek provides us with a broader understanding of the Divine nature. θεός encompasses both the concept of God as a singular Entity and gods as plural beings. This translation acknowledges the diverse beliefs and religious traditions that exist across cultures. It prompts us to explore the complexities of monotheism and polytheism and invites us to consider how our understanding of God can transcend cultural boundaries.

By examining the translations of these Divine names from Hebrew to Greek, we gain valuable insights into the theological concepts and nuances present in both the Old and New Testaments. The choice to render these names differently in Greek raises thought-provoking questions about the nature of God and our understanding of Him across different languages and cultures. As we delve deeper into this topic, we will explore how these translations have influenced religious thought and shaped our perception of Divinity throughout history.

In this book, we will embark on a comprehensive journey through biblical texts and scholarly insights to unravel the significance and implications of translating the Old Testament Divine names into Greek. We will examine various theological perspectives, historical contexts, and linguistic nuances to gain a holistic understanding of this fascinating subject matter. Through careful analysis and exploration, we hope to shed light on the complexities inherent in translating sacred texts while deepening our appreciation for the Divine names that have shaped religious traditions for centuries.

Chapter 1: Defining the Trinity

Attempting to define the Trinity can be a daunting task. Our human language and comprehension are fundamentally limited and cannot fully encapsulate the Divine mystery of God's Nature. Attempting to define the concept of the Trinity can lead us to oversimplify God's limitless and indescribable nature, confining it to the limitations of our human comprehension. This can create oversimplified or erroneous concepts that fail to honor the profound complexity and holiness of the Almighty. Although such attempts are often well-intentioned, they may inadvertently lead to misunderstandings or heresies that distort our perception of God and impair our relationship with Him. Therefore, it is essential to approach the doctrine of the Trinity with humility and reverence, recognizing that while we strive to understand the truth revealed in scripture, the fullness of God's Nature will always transcend human description and remain a sacred mystery to be respected rather than fully explained.

The very essence of God's Nature is shrouded in a profound mystery that surpasses human understanding. If we, as finite beings, could fully explain every aspect of God, including the deep and complex doctrine of the Trinity, then God's limitless, transcendent character would be undermined. The Trinity, which describes God as three distinct Persons—the Father, the Son, and the Holy Spirit—in one Divine essence, is a perfect example of such a mystery. It is a holy and ineffable union that challenges our comprehension, yet it is central to the Christian faith. This inability to completely grasp God's Nature is not a failure of our intellect but a testament to His Divine majesty. If God were fully explicable in terms of human language and thought, He wouldn't be the limitless, all-knowing Creator that the Bible describes Him as, but rather a being as limited and finite as the minds trying to understand Him. In accepting this mystery, faith finds its strength, and believers find their humility as they worship a God who is beyond the full grasp of human reason—a God who is truly God.

Warfield's definition stands out as one of the most comprehensive: it asserts that there is only one true God, yet within the unity of the Godhead, there exist three co-eternal and coequal Persons, identical in essence but distinct in existence (1930).[1] This definition affirms unity and plurality while safeguarding the equality and eternal nature of the Three. Although the term "Person" may not be ideal, it effectively prevents modalism, and the phrase "the same in substance" (or perhaps better, essence) safeguards against tritheism. God's complete and undivided essence pertains to the three Persons equally. The statement in John 10:30, "I and the Father are One," [unless otherwise noted, all Bible verses are from the King James Version] eloquently illustrates the harmony between the distinctiveness of the Persons and the unity of the essence. "I and the Father" unmistakably distinguishes two Persons, and the verb "We are" is also plural. However, the Lord declares, "We are One," and "One" is neuter, signifying unity in nature or essence, but not as one Person (which would require the masculine form). Thus, the Lord distinguishes Himself from the Father, claiming unity and equality.

Here are three examples of how people have defined the Trinity over the years and the problems associated with these definitions:

1. The States of Water:

- Water can exist in three states: liquid, solid (ice), and gas (vapor). Similarly, God is one but exists in three distinct Persons. Like water, which remains the same substance in all three states, God remains one in essence in all three manifestations.

When drawing parallels between the Trinity and the states of water, we must tread carefully to avoid inadvertently minimizing the Triune God. While the comparison to water existing as liquid, solid, and gas may help illustrate the concept of one substance in three states, it risks oversimplifying the Divine and unique relationships within the Godhead. The states of water are merely physical phases that do not possess distinct wills or relational dynamics. The Trinity, however, is not a mere form or manifestation; it embodies a much deeper unity and diversity, with each Person—Father, Son, and Holy Spirit—fully and eternally God, engaging in perfect communion and cooperative action. If not understood with the nuances of theological truth, this analogy might unintentionally imply a modalistic view. This historical heresy denies the distinct personal existence of each member of the Trinity. Thus, while seeking to make the Trinity accessible, it's vital to affirm that no earthly comparison can fully encompass the majesty and complexity of the Triune Nature of God.

1. The Sun Analogy:

- Consider the sun in the sky. It has three distinct aspects: the actual ball of gas (the sun itself), the light that emanates from it, and the heat it produces. These three elements are distinct, yet all are part of the one sun. Similarly, the Father, Son, and Holy Spirit are different from each other but all part of one God.

The Sun analogy, while attempting to illustrate the concept of the Trinity, inadvertently harms the Trinity definition. By likening the Father, Son, and Holy Spirit to the distinct aspects of the sun, it implies a hierarchy or subordination within the Trinity, which contradicts the doctrine of co-equality. The analogy suggests that the Father, Son, and Holy Spirit are analogous to the sun, its light, and its heat; with the sun being the primary entity and the light and heat being secondary. This unintentionally undermines the co-equality of the three Persons of the Trinity as taught in Christian doctrine. The Trinity doctrine affirms that the Father, Son, and Holy Spirit are co-equal and co-eternal, with each Entity being fully God and not subordinate to one another. Therefore, while the analogy may seek to clarify the concept of the Trinity, it ultimately falls short in representing the essential co-equality of the three Persons within the Godhead.

1. The Mind, Body, Spirit:

• The "Mind, Body, Spirit" analogy, while commonly used to explain the concept of the Trinity, can be considered harmful in some theological contexts. This analogy, which compares the Father, Son, and Holy Spirit to the mind, body, and spirit, can be problematic because it may lead to misunderstandings about the nature of the Trinity. The analogy of the mind, body, and spirit implies a division within God, which does not align with the traditional Christian understanding of the Trinity as three distinct Persons in one Godhead. The analogy can lead to the heresy of modalism, which denies the distinctiveness of the Father, Son, and Holy Spirit and instead suggests that They are simply different modes or manifestations of the same being. Additionally, the "Mind, Body, Spirit" analogy may inadvertently diminish the full Divinity of each Person of the Trinity.

The Trinity is not illogical; it is just unfathomable from our three dimensional perspective. On the human level, an individual is considered one being, and any two individuals are separate beings—similar to how, in two dimensions (such as on a flat sheet of paper), one square represents one figure, and any two squares represent two separate figures. On the Divine level, personalities still exist, but they are combined in ways that are beyond our imagination as inhabitants of a lower level. In God's dimension, there exists a being who is three Persons while remaining one Being, much like a cube consists of six squares while remaining a single cube. It is impossible for us to fully comprehend a Being of that nature, just as we would be unable to properly imagine a cube if we were limited to perceiving only two dimensions in space. Nonetheless, we can grasp a vague notion of it. When we do, we begin to form a faint but positive idea of something super-personal—something that transcends mere personhood (Lewis 1952).[2]

All You Need To Know

The concept of the Trinity is a mystery debated and contemplated by theologians for centuries. While it may be difficult for our finite minds to comprehend fully, it serves as a reminder of the depth and complexity of God's Nature. All we need to know is that one God exists as three distinct, co-equal, and co-eternal Persons: the Father, the Son (Jesus Christ), and the Holy Spirit. Each Person is entirely God, yet They are not separate from one another. This understanding emphasizes the unity of the three Persons in one Divine essence, which is holy. This doctrine is central to the Christian faith and is based on biblical teachings. Trying to explain more than this will almost always lead to some heretical doctrine. Trinity, or Godhead, refers to God's Divine nature and essence, encompassing the Father, Son, and Holy Spirit. If one were to say that any part of the Godhead is not God, it would be considered blasphemous. This assertion challenges the core of who God is and questions God's unity and Divinity.

Lastly, God gives us progressive revelation throughout the Bible. If someone rejects progressive revelation, that person must find all the answers about God in Genesis, such as the three days and three nights in the tomb, which are hinted at in Jonah. This is called adumbrated (foreshadow, hint, suggestion, outline partially).

Historical Emergence: Tracing the Development of Trinitarian Thought

This book explores how the concept of the Trinity has developed over time while proving the concept has always been rooted in the biblical scriptures. This concept is central to the beliefs of many Christians around the world. But understanding where it came from, how it has evolved, and why it matters, will help us appreciate the significance of the Triune God.

The early Christian texts and the Bible did not directly mention the Trinity; instead, they hinted at it rather than explicitly stating it. It was not until later that Christians began to contemplate this concept. Did they intend to label this idea? They did not aim to label God's people in a derogatory way but to facilitate identification among believers. Their effort to unite true believers was accepted, while unitarians rejected it, naturally causing a division among followers of Christ.

The first big step in shaping this concept was through debates and councils. Early church leaders and thinkers gathered to discuss and argue about the Trinity's nature. It was a hot topic because it was tough to understand how God could be three Persons but still one God. These intense discussions showed how important it was for them to get it right. One famous meeting, the Council of Nicaea in 325 AD, which we will go into in great depth in Chapter Eight, is where the Nicene Creed, a statement of faith that includes the Trinity, was created.

Over the centuries, the understanding and explanation of the Trinity developed further. Thinkers like Augustine and Thomas Aquinas made significant contributions. They tried to explain it in ways people could understand, using analogies and theological arguments. Their work helped the idea of the Trinity become more accepted and understood by Christians everywhere.

The development of Trinitarian thought has also faced challenges. Groups and individuals disagreed with the concept, arguing against it based on their interpretations of scripture and theological reasoning. These challenges have prompted further reflection and discussion, leading to a deeper understanding and more robust defense of Trinitarian doctrine.

Today, the Trinity is a core belief for many Christian denominations. It is celebrated, discussed, and crucial to worship and theology. Understanding its historical emergence helps us appreciate its complexity and significance. This journey from scriptural references to a central doctrine of faith shows the deep thought and severe reflection Christians have put into understanding their belief in God.

Tracing the development of Trinitarian thought is more than just an academic exercise. It's a journey through the history of Christian theology, reflecting how believers have wrestled with the mystery of God's Nature. This exploration invites believers and scholars alike to appreciate the depth and richness of this foundational doctrine.

Theological Significance: Why the Trinity Matters in Christian Doctrine

The Trinity shapes Christians' understanding of God as a fundamental concept in Christianity, even though it may initially appear complicated to grasp. According to Christian doctrine, the Trinity refers to the belief that God exists as three distinct Persons - the Father, the Son (Jesus Christ), and the Holy Spirit - while still being one God sharing one essence. This concept is significant because it shapes Christians' understanding of God. If someone lacks comprehension of the Trinity, they may mistakenly conclude that Jesus was created or that the Holy Spirit is not entirely God. Such misunderstandings can lead to placing faith in a created God rather than the true Triune God, who is revealed in the Bible. Without a proper understanding of the Trinity, there is a risk of misinterpreting the nature of God and unintentionally deviating from the fundamental teachings of Christianity. Therefore, it is essential to comprehend the Trinity to uphold the belief in the true Triune God as depicted in the Bible.

Why is the Trinity so important? Firstly, the concept sheds light on the central relationship in Christianity. Consider the most loving, respectful, and supportive family you can think of in your imagination. The Trinity illustrates that this type of relationship is what God embodies. God is not alone or isolated but a perfect exemplar of community and love. This teaches Christians that love and relationships are of utmost importance.

Secondly, The Trinity explains how Christians can experience God in different ways. For example, they might feel the presence of God the Father when marveling at the world's beauty, feel connected to Jesus Christ when they think about His life and teachings, and feel guided by the Holy Spirit when making decisions or when needing to be comforted in tough times. Each part of the Trinity interacts with people uniquely, but it's all still God.

The biggest reason the Trinity is vital in Christian doctrine is due to our salvation—the idea of being saved from sin and its consequences. Christians believe that God created the world, Jesus saved it through His death and resurrection, and the Holy Spirit works in people's hearts today to help them follow Jesus and grow in their faith. Each role is different, but They all work toward the same goal: *assisting people in being close to God.*

Lastly, the Trinity has much to do with how Christians live their daily lives. It encourages them to build good relationships, to love and respect others, and to find ways to show God's love within the world. The idea of the Trinity—a perfect, harmonious community—is a model for how people should treat each other. It's about being there for one another, just as God is there for everyone. The Bible instructs believers to have a unified mindset in Christ, emphasizing the importance of harmony and unity among fellow Christians. According to Philippians 2:2, "Make my joy complete by being like-minded, having the same love, being one in spirit and of one mind." This unity is established on a shared comprehension of who God is and what He means to us. It is challenging to have like-mindedness if we have differing opinions about God because our perception of Him influences our beliefs, values, and actions. Therefore, striving for a common understanding of God's Nature and character is vital in promoting authentic unity and fellowship within the body of Christ.

Subordinationism or Economic Trinity

When delving into the theological concepts of subordinationism and the Economic Trinity, it becomes essential to understand the distinction between the two and their biblical grounding within the doctrine of the Trinity.

Subordinationism historically refers to a belief system within Christian theology that suggests a form of subordination or inequality within the Trinity. This erroneous concept, which has been deemed heretical within Christian orthodoxy, presents a skewed understanding of the relationships among the Father, Son, and Holy Spirit. It often implies a hierarchy where the Son and the Holy Spirit are considered lesser in essence or being than the Father. Subordinationism can manifest in various forms, one of which is the teaching that the Son is not co-eternal or co-equal with the Father, thereby undermining the fundamental unity and equality within the Godhead.

On the other hand, the Economic Trinity is based on what the Bible says about the roles and functions of the three Persons of the Trinity—Father, Son, and Holy Spirit—in relation to the world and God's plan for salvation. This concept acknowledges the distinct roles assumed by each Person of the Trinity in the economy of redemption while affirming Their complete equality in nature and essence. The Economic Trinity highlights the cooperative work of the Father, Son, and Holy Spirit in redemptive history, without implying any subordination or inequality in Their Divine attributes.

The misunderstanding often arises from a failure to distinguish between the roles and functions of the Persons of the Trinity and any notion of inequality in its essential nature. Drawing on the analogy of the family structure, where a husband and wife fulfill distinct roles such as motherhood and fatherhood, it becomes evident that these differing roles do not imply a difference in Their human nature.

Similarly, within the Trinity, the distinct roles of the Father, Son, and Holy Spirit do not signify any inequality or subordination in Their Divine nature and attributes. Instead, they work harmoniously, each fulfilling a unique role within the Godhead while maintaining complete equality in Their Divine essence.

In conclusion, the biblical doctrine of the Trinity affirms the complete unity and equality of the Father, Son, and Holy Spirit while acknowledging Their distinct roles within the Godhead. Subordinationism, with its implications of inequality and subordination among the Persons of the Trinity, stands in contrast to the scriptural portrayal of co-equality and unity within the Godhead. On the other hand, the Economic Trinity aligns with the biblical revelation of the cooperative work of the three Persons of the Trinity in the economy of salvation, reflecting Their harmonious collaboration without compromising Their essential equality and unity.

Chapter 2: Biblical Foundations of the Trinity Old Testament

One of the most captivating mysteries in the Bible is the concept of the Trinity, which has been a topic of discussion among theologians and believers for centuries. Although the Trinity is often associated with the New Testament and the teachings of Jesus, its roots can also be traced back to the Old Testament. In this chapter, we will explore the passages and verses that allude to the existence of the Trinity in the Old Testament. We will shed light on this enigmatic doctrine at the heart of Christian belief.

The term "Trinity" is not explicitly mentioned in the Old Testament, but there are numerous instances where we can see glimpses of this Divine mystery. These passages provide hints and foreshadowing of the three Persons of God working together in perfect unity. One example can be found in Genesis 1:26, where God says, "Let us make mankind in our image, in our likeness." Using plural pronouns like "us" and "our" suggests a plurality within God's being. This hints at the existence of multiple Persons within the Divine nature, which aligns with the concept of the Trinity. Another passage that points to the Trinity can be found in Isaiah 6:8, where Isaiah hears the voice of the LORD saying, "Whom shall I send? And who will go for us?" Again, we see plural pronouns, indicating a communal dialogue within God himself. This suggests a profound relationship between multiple Persons within the Godhead.

Throughout the Old Testament, there are instances where God's Spirit is mentioned alongside God Himself. Psalm 104:30, for example, says, "When you send your Spirit, they are created." Here, we see a collaboration between God and His Spirit in the act of creation. This implies that both God and His Spirit are active participants in shaping and sustaining the world. The foundation for the doctrine of the Trinity was laid even before Jesus walked on Earth. The Old Testament provides us with glimpses and foreshadowings of this profound mystery, paving the way for its fuller revelation in the New Testament.

This chapter will explore the significance of several Old Testament passages in understanding the Trinity. By analyzing these ancient texts through a Trinitarian lens, we can better appreciate the timeless truths woven into Scripture since its earliest beginnings. We will also delve into how these glimpses of the Trinity in the Old Testament set the stage for Jesus' teachings on His relationship with the Father and the Holy Spirit. Through careful study and reflection on these passages, we hope to gain a renewed appreciation for the depth and complexity of our faith and how the Trinity has been present from ancient times until now.

Hidden from the Devil and his minions

God, in His infinite wisdom, has a way of concealing His bigger plan from the Devil. Throughout the Bible, we see glimpses of this Divine strategy, where God strategically hides His intentions and purposes from the enemy. This showcases God's sovereignty and highlights His power and wisdom over all creation. In Matthew 13:11, Jesus says, "To you, it has been given to know the secrets of the kingdom of heaven, but to them, it has not been given." Through this verse, we understand that God chooses to reveal His plans to those who have a genuine heart for Him while keeping the enemy in the dark.

One of the prime examples of God hiding His bigger plan from the Devil can be found in the story of Jesus' crucifixion and resurrection. The Devil believed that by orchestrating Jesus' death on the cross, he had triumphed and won a great victory. Little did he know that God had a much greater plan in motion. 1 Corinthians 2:7-8 is written, "But we impart a secret and hidden wisdom of God, which God decreed before the ages for our glory. None of the rulers of this age understood this, for if they had, they would not have crucified the Lord of glory." Here, we see that if Satan had known the full extent of God's plan, he would have never allowed Jesus to be crucified because it ultimately led to his defeat and our redemption.

Another example can be seen in the book of Genesis when Joseph was sold into slavery by his brothers. Joseph's journey was filled with hardships and trials, but little did he know that God used these circumstances to position him as a powerful ruler in Egypt. In Genesis 50:20, Joseph tells his brothers, "As for you, you meant evil against me, but God meant it for good." This verse reveals that even though Joseph's brothers had evil intentions, God had a more excellent plan. He used their actions to fulfill His purpose and elevate Joseph to a position where he could save his family and many others from famine.

Yet another example is when the devil challenges Jesus to prove His identity as the Son of God by turning stones into bread.[3] Although Jesus could have easily performed this miracle, He chose to keep His Divine power hidden from the Devil at that moment, despite the Devil's recognition of His Divine authority.

Proverbs 21:30 states, "No wisdom, no understanding, no counsel can avail against the LORD." This verse emphasizes that no matter how cunning or strategic the Devil may be, he cannot outsmart or thwart God's plans. The enemy may think he has gained an advantage, but God's purposes will ultimately prevail. This truth is further reinforced in Isaiah 55:8-9, which says, "For my thoughts are not your thoughts, neither are your ways my ways... For as the heavens are higher than the earth, so are my ways higher than your ways and my thoughts than your thoughts." These verses remind us that God's ways are far beyond our comprehension and that He is always working behind the scenes to fulfill His greater plan.

God has a remarkable ability to hide His bigger plan from the Devil. We can see how God strategically conceals His intentions from the enemy through various biblical accounts and verses. This highlights His sovereignty and showcases His power and wisdom over all creation. As believers, we can take comfort in knowing that no matter how complex or confusing our circumstances may seem, God is always at work behind the scenes, orchestrating His perfect plan for our lives.

However, when someone is actively engaging in doing the will of the devil, intentionally or unintentionally, it can greatly hinder their understanding of who Jesus really is. The devil, being the ultimate deceiver, seeks to blind individuals from the truth and keep them in darkness. Similarly, if someone is willingly following the plans and desires of the devil, their ability to recognize and comprehend the true nature of Jesus may be obstructed. Just as God hides certain things from the devil, those entangled in the devil's will may find themselves unable to perceive the light and truth that Jesus represents. Only by turning away from the devil's influence and seeking a genuine relationship with Jesus can one truly understand and embrace His Divine nature.

Seeking The Kingdom

The book of Proverbs[4] reveals that God sometimes hides things from us. At first, this might seem confusing or discouraging since we all want to understand what's happening in our lives. However, if we think deeper about this idea, we can see that God doesn't hide things to make our lives harder. Instead, He wants us to seek Him more actively so that we can find the extraordinary truths and blessings that He has in store for us.

When we face challenges or uncertainties, it's easy to become frustrated or disheartened. We may question why God chooses to conceal certain things from us. However, it's important to remember that God's ways are higher than ours, and His thoughts are higher than ours. He sees the bigger picture and knows what's best for us. In His wisdom, He may choose to conceal some things for a while to strengthen our faith and reliance on Him. God has never concealed salvation from anyone. It is a gift[5] to the whole world, and salvation is found in one place only: God Jesus!

But God doesn't want us to remain in a state of confusion or ignorance forever. The book of Hebrews tells us that God rewards those diligently seeking Him. This means that when we actively pursue a deeper relationship with God and seek His guidance, He will reveal Himself to us and grant us understanding. Through this diligent search, we can discover the truth and experience the rewards of a close and intimate relationship with our Creator.

Diligently seeking God requires patience, perseverance, and faith. It may involve praying, studying His Word, seeking wise counsel, and listening for His voice in our hearts. It's not always easy, but the rewards[6] far outweigh the effort required. As we seek God diligently, we grow closer to Him, all the while gaining wisdom and discernment.

God delights in revealing Himself to those who earnestly seek Him. Just as a loving parent delights in sharing secrets with their child, God longs to share His wisdom and knowledge with us. He wants us to experience the joy of discovering His truth and walking in His ways. The rewards of diligently seeking God are not only spiritual but also practical. We gain insight into life's challenges, find peace amidst chaos, and receive direction for our paths.

So, let us not be discouraged when God chooses to conceal a matter from us. Instead, let us be encouraged to diligently seek Him, knowing He rewards those who earnestly pursue Him. Let us trust in His timing and wisdom, knowing He has a purpose for every season of concealment. And as we continue on this journey of faith, may we be open to the treasures that await us as we uncover the hidden truths God has prepared for those who diligently seek Him.

Hermeneutical Bible Study

Hermeneutics is a branch of knowledge that deals with interpreting and understanding texts, particularly ancient and religious texts. It provides a systematic approach to understanding the meaning and significance of these texts, allowing readers to gain insight into the author's intentions and the cultural context in which the text was written. In Bible study, hermeneutics enables readers to interpret and apply the teachings within its pages.

To apply hermeneutics to Bible study, one must first recognize the importance of understanding the historical and cultural background of the biblical text. This involves studying the social, political, and religious context in which the text was written, as well as the author's language, literary style, and genre. By doing so, one can gain valuable insights into the passage's original meaning and intent.

Another critical aspect of applying hermeneutics to Bible study is approaching the text with an open mind and a willingness to engage with it critically. This means carefully examining the content of the text, paying attention to details such as repeated words or phrases, rhetorical devices, and the passage's structure. It also involves comparing and contrasting different passages within the Bible to gain a deeper understanding of their interconnectedness and overarching themes.

Furthermore, hermeneutics encourages readers to consider the broader theological framework within the text. This involves reflecting on how the passage relates to other biblical doctrines and teachings and its implications for one's faith and practice. Individuals can better understand the text and its relevance to their lives today by engaging in this holistic approach to Bible study.

However, it must be noted that hermeneutics can be used correctly but it can also be misused. A wrong way to use hermeneutics in Bible study would be to approach the text with preconceived biases or agendas. This could involve cherry-picking verses or passages that support one's own beliefs while ignoring or dismissing those that challenge them. Such an approach not only distorts the text's original meaning but also fails to engage with its fullness and richness.

On the other hand, an excellent way to use hermeneutics in Bible study is to strive for an objective and balanced interpretation of the text. This requires humility, openness, and a commitment to approaching the text with intellectual integrity. It also involves seeking guidance from reputable scholars, consulting various commentaries and resources, and engaging in dialogue with others with different perspectives. By doing so, individuals can ensure that their interpretation is grounded in the sound principles of hermeneutics and is faithful to the original message of the biblical text.

Hermeneutics provides a valuable framework for interpreting and understanding ancient texts such as the Bible. By applying hermeneutical principles to Bible study, individuals can gain a deeper appreciation for its historical and cultural context, engage with its content critically, and discern its theological implications. However, it is essential to use hermeneutics responsibly and avoid subjective interpretations that distort or misrepresent the text's original meaning.

When studying the Bible, using a consistent hermeneutical framework is essential. Hermeneutics is the science of interpreting biblical texts, and it helps us understand the intended meaning behind the words. However, many people make the mistake of disregarding certain teachings just because specific words are not explicitly mentioned in the Bible. *One example of this is the concept of the Trinity.*

The word "Trinity" may not be found in the Bible, but that does not mean that the teaching itself is heresy or invalid. In fact, many Christian theologians and scholars have derived the doctrine of the

Trinity from various passages throughout the Bible. The Trinity refers to believing in one God who exists in three Persons: Father, Son, and Holy Spirit. While the word may not be present, the concept is evident in passages such as Matthew 28:19, where Jesus commands His disciples to baptize in the name of the Father, Son, and Holy Spirit.

It's essential to recognize that not all biblical teachings are explicitly mentioned by name. Just because a specific word is not present, it doesn't mean that the underlying concept or truth is not there. For example, when describing God, the Bible does not explicitly mention attributes like omnipresence, omniscience, and omnipotence. However, through careful study and examination of various passages, we can understand that these attributes are indeed ascribed to God. Those who reject the concept of the trinity because the word "trinity" is not found in scripture often believe in a unitarian God. However, the word "unitarian" is also not found in scripture. One step further, I would be willing to bet that these same people will use the word "Bible" to define the canon, the Old Testament, and the New Testament as a whole. The word "Bible" is not in the Bible.

Therefore, when studying the Bible, it's crucial to approach each passage within a consistent hermeneutical framework. Hermeneutics helps us interpret and understand the intended meaning of the text. If we constantly change our hermeneutics from one passage to another, our understanding of doctrine will be built on shaky ground.

Consistency in hermeneutics allows us to apply the same principles of interpretation across different passages and books of the Bible. This ensures we do not cherry-pick verses or disregard teachings based on our biases or preferences. We can uncover deeper truths and gain a more comprehensive understanding of God's word by employing proper hermeneutics.

It's foolish to disregard a biblical teaching or concept simply because specific words like "Trinity" are not explicitly mentioned in the Bible. The absence of particular words does not negate the validity of a doctrine or concept. Just as we recognize attributes like omnipresence and omniscience without specific mention in scripture, we must consistently approach all teachings and employ proper hermeneutics. Doing so builds a solid foundation for understanding God's word and helps us to avoid being swayed by personal interpretations or biases.

Old Testament Echoes of a Triune God

Several instances in the Old Testament mention YHVH, the Angel of YHVH, and the Spirit of YHVH. These references echo the Trinity concept found in the New Testament: the Father, Son, and Holy Spirit.

Firstly, YHVH is the Hebrew name for God, often translated as "the LORD" in English translations. Throughout the Old Testament, YHVH is portrayed as the sovereign and all-powerful God who created and sustains the universe. In the New Testament, Jesus Christ is revealed as the Son of God, who shares the same Divine essence as the Father.[7] This aligns with the concept of YHVH representing God the Father.

Secondly, the Angel of YHVH appears in various Old Testament narratives as a Divine messenger sent by God to interact with humans. This angel is often described as having Divine attributes and authority, and some scholars believe He is a pre-incarnate appearance of Jesus Christ. In the New Testament, Jesus is sometimes referred to as the "Angel of the Lord".[8] This parallel between the Angel of YHVH and Jesus Christ further strengthens the connection between the Old Testament and New Testament representations of God.

Lastly, the Spirit of YHVH is mentioned throughout the Old Testament as the Divine presence who empowers individuals for specific tasks or roles. In the New Testament, the Holy Spirit is portrayed as a distinct Person within the Godhead who indwells believers and empowers them for ministry.[9] The Spirit of YHVH in the Old Testament foreshadows the role of the Holy Spirit in the New Testament, highlighting Their shared Divine nature.

Elohim

Starting with Genesis 1:1 is an excellent way to search for the presence of the Holy Trinity in the Old Testament. This verse lays the foundation for understanding the role of the Holy Trinity in creation, establishing God as the ultimate authority and source of all things. However, when translated into another language, we miss something important in the original language.

In Hebrew, "Elohim" is derived from the root word "El," which means God or Deity. However, unlike other words for God in the Bible, such as Yahweh or Adonai, Elohim is always used in the plural. This has led scholars and theologians to ponder its meaning for centuries.

One interpretation is that Elohim reflects the majestic nature of God. Using a plural form, the Old Testament emphasizes God's power, authority, and greatness. It signifies that God is not limited to a single Entity but encompasses all aspects of Divinity. In this sense, *Elohim* conveys awe-inspiring grandeur and magnificence.

Another interpretation suggests that Elohim hints at God's complex nature. While it may seem contradictory for a singular God to be described in the plural form, it highlights the Divine's multifaceted characteristics. Just as a diamond sparkles with various facets, so does God possess multiple attributes and qualities. Elohim reminds us that God is not easily defined nor is He confined to our limited understanding.

Furthermore, some scholars argue that the plural form of Elohim suggests the presence of a Divine council or heavenly assembly. This concept aligns with ancient Near Eastern cultures, where kings would gather advisors and courtiers to assist in decision-making. Similarly, Elohim could imply that God governs alongside other heavenly beings who carry out His will. There is no biblical evidence that God ordered or commanded anything called Elohim to create anything whatsoever. The Bible only makes it clear that He had entities acting as His agents to deliver messages. They are dispatched to protect and guard God's people[10] or deliver messages, for example—Gabriel to Mary or Gabriel to Daniel.

Interestingly, this idea of a Divine council finds limited support in several passages in the Old Testament. For instance, Psalm 82:1 says, "God presides in the great assembly; he renders judgment among the gods." Here, "gods" refers to Divine beings who serve under God's authority. Similarly, in Genesis 1:26, God says, "Let us make mankind in our image." Using "us" suggests a collective decision-making process among Divine beings.

However, it's important to note that these interpretations are not universally accepted. Some scholars argue that the plural form of Elohim may be a grammatical artifact or simply a way to show reverence and respect for God. They believe Elohim should be understood as a singular noun with plural attributes rather than a literal plurality. The problem is that Elohim is used to identify angels and humans. If it was to show respect for God, should we also imply the same hermeneutics and show respect to fallen angels? I think not!

Elohim is used over 2,500 times in the Old Testament. Its consistent use in the plural form raises intriguing questions about God's Nature and relationship with other Divine beings. Whether reflecting God's majesty, complexity, or involvement with a heavenly council, Elohim adds depth and richness to our understanding of the Divine. Ultimately, it reminds us that while we may struggle to comprehend the fullness of God's Nature, we can find comfort and wonder in His vast and mysterious existence.

My Stand on Elohim

The Bible contains numerous verses that teach us about the creation of the heavens and the earth. One of the most prominent teachings is that God spoke the heavens and earth into existence. In the book of Genesis, it is written, "In the beginning, God created the heavens and the earth" (Genesis 1:1). This verse establishes that God is the creator of everything we see around us. It suggests that through His powerful words, "LET THERE BE,"[11] God brought forth the entire universe.

Many verses throughout the Bible support this idea of God speaking creation into existence. For instance, Psalm 33:6 states, "By the word of the LORD, the heavens were made, their starry host by the breath of his mouth." Here, we can see that God's word can create and shape the heavens and all that dwells within them. Similarly, Hebrews 11:3 says, "Through faith we understand that the worlds were framed by the word of God, so that things which are seen were not made of things which do appear.." This verse emphasizes that God's command and His spoken word were instrumental in bringing about the creation of the universe.

These verses highlight God's incredible power and authority. They remind us that God brought everything we know today into existence through His spoken word, a testament to His Divine nature and creative abilities. Moreover, these teachings also emphasize the importance of faith and belief in God's word. By acknowledging and embracing His role as the creator, we can find meaning and purpose in our own lives.

Creator(s)

So, who created the heavens and earth? The answer can be found in the Bible. In particular, Psalms 102:25 credits God the Father with the act of creation, stating that He laid the earth's foundations and created the heavens.

But the story does not end there. In Colossians 1:16, credit for creation is also given to God the Son. This passage declares that all things were created through Jesus Christ and for Him. This highlights Jesus's role in the act of creation, suggesting that He was not only present but actively involved in bringing the world into existence.

Furthermore, the Holy Spirit is also given credit for creation in Genesis 1:2 and Job 26:13. In Genesis 1:2, it is stated that the Spirit of God was hovering over the waters at the time of creation. This suggests that the Holy Spirit was present at the very beginning, participating in the act of creation alongside God the Father and God the Son. Similarly, Job 26:13 describes how God's Spirit has adorned the heavens with His hand, further emphasizing the Holy Spirit's role in the universe's creation.

When we consider these passages together, it becomes clear that all three members of the Godhead—God the Father, God the Son, and God the Holy Spirit—are credited with the act of creation. This suggests unity and collaboration within the Trinity, with each Person contributing to and playing a vital role in bringing about the world as we know it.

This idea of a Triune God is further supported by Genesis 1:1, which states, "In the beginning, God created the heavens and the earth." The use of "God" in this verse is a translation of "Elohim" in Hebrew, which is plural in form. Many scholars have interpreted this as an indication of the Trinity, with God existing as three Persons in one being.

When we examine various passages in the Bible which discuss creation, we find that credit is given to all three members of the Trinity – God the Father, God the Son, and God the Holy Spirit. Each Person is recognized for Their role in bringing about the world as we know it today. This points to a unified and collaborative effort within the Godhead and lends credence to the belief in the Trinity. The concept of a Triune God is supported by these verses and provides a deeper understanding of how creation came to be.

In my apologetic book *Divine Revelation: Unveiling Jesus as God*, I point out that Hebrew does not have only singular and plural. Hebrew also has a dual word.

> "In English, we distinguish between singular (one) and plural (two or more). However, Hebrew operates differently. In Hebrew, they have singular (such as the word "El"[12] for God), dual (like the word "qeren"[13] for horns on an Ox), which denotes two, and plural (such as the word "Elohim"[14] for God), which represents three or more. This unique feature of the Hebrew language allows for a more nuanced expression of quantity and adds depth to their linguistic structure."[15]

In the book of Ecclesiastes 12:1, there is an intriguing use of the word "Creator" that catches the attention of many readers. This verse states, "Remember your Creator in the days of your youth." This particular use of the word "creator" is fascinating because it is in the plural form in the original language, Hebrew. Instead of referring to just one creator, it implies the existence of multiple creators. This use of the plural form raises questions and opens up a world of possibilities when it comes to understanding the concept of creation. The interpretation of this plural form of "creator" is that it represents a collective, or group effort, in creation. It suggests that creation is not solely the work of one Divine being but a collaborative process involving multiple Entities.

As you can see, my stance is simple: God is not a God of confusion. He says what He means and means what He says. God would not use a plural word for Himself and expect a layperson to understand that it is not really plural but singular. Even though "Elohim" is always plural, God would not use it to confuse people. Instead, God uses "Elohim" to emphasize His Triunecharacteristics. God could have used an absolute singular word in Hebrew, but He did not. *He **did not** for a reason.* The reason God could not use a singular word to reference Himself is because *He is triune.*

Midrash

The Midrashic tradition developed over several centuries, with its origins dating back to the Second Temple period and continuing through the early medieval era. It is an ancient collection of Jewish texts, referring to a method of interpreting biblical texts within Judaism. It involves exploring and elaborating on the stories, laws, and teachings in the Hebrew Bible (Old Testament) through various texts, including commentaries, stories, and homilies. The aim is to provide a deeper understanding and insight into the biblical narratives and their relevance to everyday life, often through storytelling, ethical teachings, and creative interpretation. The Midrash states that this Spirit of the Lord that is spoken of in Isaiah as resting upon the Messiah is the same Spirit of the Lord that moved over the primeval waters of Creation: "The Spirit of God was moving over the surface of the waters." This was the Spirit of Messiah as it is written, "The Spirit of the Lord will rest on him" (Genesis Rabbah 1:2, 6th Century CE).

We see that during Second Temple literature, the Jewish people were teaching the plurality of God. It wasn't until Jesus made the scene that they started rejecting the plurality of God because of their hatred for Jesus. However, we remember Jesus walking into the synagogue. He opened the scroll of Isaiah 61:1, which is recorded in Luke 4:18:

> "The spirit of the Lord is upon me because he anointed me to bring good news to the poor. He has sent me to proclaim release to captives, and recovery of sight to the blind, to set free those who are oppressed," (NASB).

Held Accountable

In Romans 1:18-22, the Apostle Paul reveals that God will hold people accountable for acknowledging Him as the Creator of all things. This passage emphasizes the importance of recognizing the Divine origin of everything in the world, from mountains' grandeur to a flower's intricacy. All of creation testifies[16] to the existence of God, a Creator who carefully designed and crafted every living being. Through this breathtaking display of creation, God reveals Himself to humanity, leaving us without excuse for not acknowledging His existence.

The Creator God mentioned in Romans 1:18-22 is the same Godhead found in Genesis 1:1, who spoke the universe into existence. This verse sets the foundation for understanding the nature of our Creator, as it states, "In the beginning, God created the heavens and the earth." This declaration reveals that God is not a passive observer or a distant Deity but an active participant in the creation of all things. He is the source of life, the author of everything we see and experience. Creation's intricate beauty and complexity bear witness to His wisdom, power, and creativity.

Moreover, having a genuine relationship with the Creator God goes beyond simply acknowledging His existence. It involves comprehending His Triune Nature. The concept of the Trinity is not explicitly mentioned in Romans 1:18-22, but it becomes evident as we delve deeper into Scripture. The Triune Nature of God refers to the Father, Son, and Holy Spirit existing as three distinct Persons yet one God. This Divine mystery is beautifully revealed throughout the Bible, from Genesis to Revelation.

Understanding God's Triune Nature has practical implications for our faith and relationship with Him. It enables us to experience a deeper intimacy with Him as we approach Him as our loving Father who cares for us, as Jesus Christ who sacrificed Himself for our salvation, and as the Holy Spirit who guides and empowers us daily. *Appreciating God's multifaceted character enriches our worship and strengthens our faith.*

Romans 1:18-22 reminds us that God will hold us accountable for knowing Him as the Creator God. The evidence of creation is all around us, bearing witness to His existence and power. As we study Scripture, we discover that this Creator God is the Triune Godhead found in Genesis 1:1. Through a genuine relationship with Him, we know and experience His Triune Nature - Father, Son, and Holy Spirit. May our hearts be open to recognizing and embracing this truth, for it is through understanding and knowing our Creator that we can find fulfillment and purpose in life.

Caution

In a world filled with countless beliefs and religions, it is of utmost importance to caution people to study the Bible and know the real God. Many individuals hold onto their faith without truly understanding within Whom they are placing their trust. They may have a vague notion of a higher power or a god, but if this perception is not grounded in the teachings of the Bible, their faith could easily be misplaced. It is crucial to distinguish between the real God as revealed in the Bible, and every other god not found within its pages.

The Bible is a guidebook for those seeking a genuine relationship with God. It contains His words, teachings, and promises. By studying the Bible, we can gain insight into His character, His desires for our lives, and His plans for our salvation. *Without this knowledge, our faith becomes vulnerable to misconceptions and distortions.* We risk putting our trust in a god who may be shaped by human interpretation or cultural influences rather than the true God. No one wants to hear, "I never knew you; LEAVE ME."[17]

One might wonder why it is so important to know the real God of the Bible. The answer lies in the fact that salvation is at stake. If we place our faith in a god that is not found in the Bible, we are essentially putting our trust in something or someone who cannot save us. As revealed in the Bible, the real God is the only one with the power to bring about true salvation and eternal life. By knowing Him intimately through His Word, we can be assured that our faith is in the right hands.

Furthermore, knowing the real God of the Bible allows us to experience a deeper and more meaningful relationship with Him. We can develop a genuine love and trust for God when we understand His character and His ways. The Bible reveals His attributes: love, mercy, righteousness, and justice. It shows us how He has interacted with humanity throughout history and how He desires a personal relationship with each of us. By studying the Bible, we can align our understanding of God with who He truly is rather than relying on hearsay, popular opinion, or a created Jesus that is not found in the scriptures.

It is crucial to approach studying the Bible with an open mind and a humble heart. We must set aside our preconceived notions and allow God to reveal Himself to us through His Word. It may be challenging at times to grapple with certain concepts or teachings, but with prayer and guidance from the Holy Spirit, we can gain a deeper understanding of who God truly is.

In conclusion, cautioning people to study the Bible in order that they come to know the real God is crucial for their faith journey. Placing our trust in a god that is not found in the pages of Scripture can lead to misguided beliefs and missed opportunities for salvation.

By investing time and effort into studying the Bible, we can develop a genuine and authentic relationship with the real God, who has the power to save us and transform our lives. So let us dive into its pages with an open heart and mind, ready to encounter the real God who longs for us to know Him intimately.

Deuteronomy 6:4

Deuteronomy 6:4 is a verse that has captivated scholars for centuries. The verse reads as follows: "Hear, O Israel: The LORD our God, the LORD [all capitalization emphasis added] is one." The use of the tetragrammaton, LORD, YHWH, which represents the personal name of God, emphasizes the singularity and uniqueness of the LORD. However, what is fascinating is the choice of the word "God" in this verse. It is Elohim, a plural form of the word god. This seemingly contradictory combination holds a deep significance and provides a glimpse into the concept of the Trinity. The frequent usage of the combined name Yahweh Elohim highlights that God is not just the Maker but also the covenant God who establishes a relationship with His creation (Alexander and Baker 2003, 286).[18]

In the New Testament, Jesus is revealed as the covenant God. Throughout the Bible, God made covenants with His people to establish His relationship with them and to provide salvation and redemption. In the Old Testament, God made a covenant with Abraham, promising to bless him and his descendants. This covenant was fulfilled in Jesus, who came from the lineage of Abraham. Matthew 1:1 states, "The book of the genealogy of Jesus Christ, the Son of David, the Son of Abraham." This verse establishes Jesus as the fulfillment of God's covenant with Abraham.

Furthermore, Jesus Himself spoke of His identity as the covenant God. In Luke 22:20, during the Last Supper, Jesus said, "This cup is the new covenant in my blood, which is poured out for you." Here, Jesus clearly identifies His blood as the sign and symbol of a new covenant. This statement emphasizes that Jesus is the mediator of this new covenant and is its very foundation.

The significance of Jesus' blood as the covenant is further emphasized in Hebrews 9:14-15, which states, "How much more will the blood of Christ... cleanse our consciences from acts that lead to death so that we may serve the living God! For this reason, Christ is the mediator of a new covenant." This passage underscores that it is through Jesus' blood that our sins are forgiven and our relationship with God is restored. It also highlights Jesus' role as the mediator and guarantor of this new covenant.

The New Testament clearly portrays Jesus as the covenant God. Through Him, God's promises to His people are fulfilled. Jesus Himself identified His blood as the sign and symbol of this new covenant. Through His blood, our sins are forgiven and our relationship with God is restored. The New Testament reaffirms that Jesus is not only the mediator but also the very foundation of this covenant.

The usage of the word Elohim in conjunction with the singular LORD reveals a profound mystery about God's Nature. The Trinity consists of three Persons - God the Father, God the Son, and God the Holy Spirit - who are distinct yet inseparable. While Deuteronomy 6:4 does not explicitly mention these three Persons, it lays the foundation for this theological understanding.

The plural form, Elohim, signifies the plurality within the Godhead. It hints at the existence of multiple Persons within the Divine nature. Just as Elohim implies a plurality within a singular Entity, so does the concept of the Trinity imply multiple Persons within one God. The Father, Son, and Holy Spirit are eternally united in perfect harmony and coexistence, each playing a unique role in creation and redemption. When we contemplate Deuteronomy 6:4 and its connection to the Trinity, we are reminded that God is not limited by our human understanding or confined to our earthly concepts of singularity.

The Trinity is a Divine mystery that surpasses our comprehension, but it is an essential aspect of our faith. As believers, we can take comfort in knowing that our God is not distant or detached from us. He is intimately involved in our lives and desires a personal relationship with each one of us. The Trinity reveals that God is not only powerful and majestic but also compassionate and relatable. We have a loving Father who sent His Son to redeem us and His Holy Spirit to guide and empower us.

Deuteronomy 6:4 reminds us that our faith is rooted in a God who is beyond our understanding. We may not fully grasp the intricacies of the Trinity, but we can trust in the truth it represents—that our God is one in essence and yet exists in three distinct Persons. It is through this Divine mystery that we experience the fullness of God's love, grace, and salvation.

Deuteronomy 6:4 beautifully highlights both the singularity and plurality within God's Nature. The tetragrammaton YHWH emphasizes the oneness of the LORD, while the word Elohim hints at the plurality within the Divine being. While this verse does not explicitly mention the Trinity, it sets the stage for understanding this fundamental aspect of our faith. The Trinity reveals that our God is not only powerful but also personal, inviting us into a relationship with Him. Let us embrace this beautiful mystery and continue to explore its depths as we grow in our understanding of who God truly is.

Echad

In Hebrew, the word "echad" denotes the number one. Interestingly, in Deuteronomy 6:4, this word is employed with the plural noun "Elohim" and the singular noun "LORD." This verse, known as the Shema, has been a central tenet of Jewish faith for centuries. It states, "Hear, O Israel: The LORD our God, the LORD is one." The use of "echad" in this context has led theologians and scholars to speculate on its significance and implications for understanding God's Nature.

Including the plural noun "Elohim" alongside the singular noun "LORD" in Deuteronomy 6:4 has led many to interpret this verse as a reference to the Trinity. "Elohim" is a common Hebrew term used throughout the Old Testament to refer to God. As I have discussed previously, its plural form has sparked debate among scholars, with some arguing that it suggests a plurality within the Godhead. The use of "echad" in this verse can be seen as supporting this interpretation, as it implies a unity within the plurality.

If God had wanted to convey an absolute singular sense, He could have used the Hebrew word "El." This word is also used in the Old Testament to refer to God, but it carries a connotation of singularity. However, in Deuteronomy 6:4, God chose to use the word "echad," which suggests unity within the Godhead despite the plurality expressed by "Elohim." This has led many theologians to see this verse affirming God's Triune nature.

The use of "echad" in conjunction with the plural "Elohim" and singular "LORD" in Deuteronomy 6:4 aligns with this understanding. It suggests that while there is a plurality within the Godhead, a fundamental unity also transcends this plurality.

Common Counterargument

Some may argue that the plural term for God, Elohim, refers specifically to Israel as the verse begins with "Hear, O Israel." However, the context of the verse is about defining who and what God is. While it is true that Israel is being addressed in the verse, *the main focus is on the nature of God.* The critics' error lies in their presuppositions, or failure to truly understand the context and meaning of Deuteronomy 6:4. This verse is not about God's relationship with anyone, let alone Israel. It focuses solely on God Himself and His nature as the one true God. The plural form of Elohim does not indicate multiple gods or a Divine council. Instead, it reflects God's majestic and all-encompassing nature.

Dr. Tigay, a Jewish scholar, says despite his familiarity with the words LORD and Elohim, the exact meaning of the Shema is unclear and allows for multiple interpretations. The current translation suggests that the verse describes the correct relationship between YHVH and Israel: He alone is the God of Israel. This does not assert monotheism, which means believing in only one God (2003).[19]

May I suggest that God says what He means and means what He says! When God speaks, we do not need to try to decode some supernatural language. No, when God uses a plural word, it simply means what it says. It's not some hidden message or secret code that we have to figure out. We don't need to play guessing games with God's words because He is clear and straightforward.

In a world where deception and cunning are prevalent, the fact that God is entirely transparent in His communication is genuinely remarkable. We often find ourselves surrounded by people who twist their words, manipulate others, and try to deceive for their own personal gain. But God, in His perfect character, stands above all of that. He is honest and truthful, never playing games with our minds or leading us astray.

We need to remember that we should allow God to speak for Himself. We shouldn't try to tell God what He means or reinterpret His words to fit our desires or agenda. God's words are powerful and authoritative and should be taken at face value. When God uses a plural word, He doesn't expect us to somehow magically know that it's singular. No, He means exactly what He says.

To suggest otherwise would be to accuse God of being deceitful and cunning, which goes against His very nature. God is a God of truth and integrity and would never play tricks on His children. He wants us to understand His message clearly and follow Him wholeheartedly. So, let's not try to twist His words or manipulate their meaning to suit our own purposes. Instead, let's listen attentively to what God is saying *and trust His words are true.*

We can rest assured knowing that when God speaks, He says what He means and means what He says. We don't need to decipher some hidden code or seek secret meanings. God's words are clear and straightforward, and we should allow Him to speak for Himself. He will not use a plural word and expect us to know it's singular. That would be deceitful and cunning, which goes against His character. So, let's embrace the honesty and transparency of God's communication and trust in the truth of His words.

First Commandment

The first commandment, "You shall have no other gods before Me,"[20] is a powerful statement that highlights the existence of other gods while simultaneously asserting that God is the only true God. This commandment serves as a reminder that God is a jealous God, desiring exclusive worship and devotion from His followers. Jesus declared this commandment the greatest,[21] emphasizing the importance of giving our undivided attention and reverence to God alone. By placing this commandment as the first in the list, God establishes His position as the ultimate authority and the sole Deity deserving of our devotion.

The purpose of the First Commandment is to establish a clear and exclusive relationship between humanity and the one true God. It reminds us that no other gods or idols can take precedence over our devotion to God. *This commandment urges us to reject any form of worship or idolatry that may distract us from our relationship with God.* It is a call to wholeheartedly commit ourselves to the worship and service of the one true God.

In a world filled with various belief systems and gods, the First Commandment is a guiding principle for believers. It calls for a complete surrender and allegiance to God alone, setting Him apart from any other Deity or idol that may tempt us. By adhering to this commandment, we acknowledge God's supreme authority and sovereignty over our lives. We acknowledge His role as the creator and sustainer of all things, deserving of our unwavering devotion.

The first commandment also reminds us of God's jealousy. It emphasizes His desire for an exclusive relationship with His people, free from distractions or competing allegiances. This jealousy stems from His love for us and His desire to protect us from the harmful consequences of worshiping false gods. God knows that only He can fulfill our deepest needs and provide true fulfillment, and therefore, He calls us to turn away from any other form of worship and place our trust solely in Him.

It is unreasonable to believe that God used a plural form of a word to describe Himself and that He does not mean what He says. This misconception stems from a misunderstanding of language and grammar. Using a plural word to describe God does not imply that He is multiple beings but serves as a linguistic tool to emphasize His plural nature into one essence.

Man Created

Genesis 1:26-27 is a significant passage that supports the belief that God created man in His image. This passage states, "Then God said, 'Let us make mankind in our image, in our likeness, so that they may rule over the fish in the sea and the birds in the sky, over the livestock and all the wild animals, and over all the creatures that move along the ground.' So God created mankind in his own image, in the image of God he created them; male and female he created them."[22]

The use of plural words in Genesis 1:27, such as "us" and "our," suggests that God is a trinity. This indicates that there is plurality within God's Nature. In this passage, we see a glimpse of this Triune Nature of God.

Josephus, a first-century Jewish historian, says that after the seventh day, Moses philosophically discusses the creation of man, stating that God formed man from dust and infused him with a spirit and a soul. The man was named Adam, meaning "one that is red" in Hebrew, symbolizing his creation from the red earth, which is considered pure and genuine (Josephus and Whiston, 1987).[23]

In addition, Genesis 2:7 confirms that only God created man from the dust. The verse reads, "Then the LORD God formed a man from the dust of the ground and breathed into his nostrils the breath of life, and the man became a living being". This verse highlights that God exclusively carried out creation without anyone else being involved. It is necessary to note that no angel or other being assisted in this act of creation. If someone claimed that angels or other beings assisted in the creation of man, they would need to identify these angels or other beings' attributes, "image," or "likeness" and connect them to man.

Numerous references to angels throughout the Bible provide insight into their appearance and nature. One such description is found in the book of Ezekiel, where the prophet describes cherubim, a type of angelic being, as having four faces—that of a lion, an ox, an eagle, and a human.[24] This imagery suggests that angels possess a multidimensional nature, transcending the limitations of the human form. Another depiction of angels can be found in the book of Isaiah, where the prophet describes seraphim as having six wings - two covering their faces, two covering their feet, and two for flying.[25] This description highlights the celestial nature of angels, emphasizing their ability to move swiftly and effortlessly through different dimensions. Therefore, since we do not have any record of humans with four faces, a multidimensional nature, and six wings, it would be safe to say humans were created in God's image.

The concept of discerning the Trinity of the Unity and the Unity of the Trinity, as well as the plural and singular references in the creation of man and the likeness to God, is discussed in St. Augustine's Confessions (Augustine of Hippo 1912).[26] St. Augustine, and many, *if not all,* early church fathers teach that God is the sole creator of man.

Lastly, God created man in His likeness and image, but it is important to note that this does not mean that man is identical to God in every aspect. While man possesses certain qualities that reflect God's Nature, such as power, knowledge, morality, and unity; fundamental differences distinguish man from God.

Man is powerful, but God is all-powerful. God has given man a certain level of power and authority, allowing him to make decisions and exercise dominion over the earth. However, this power is limited and finite. On the other hand, God is omnipotent, possessing infinite power and control over all creation. His power is unrivaled and beyond human comprehension.

Man is knowledgeable, but God is all-knowing. Man has the capacity for knowledge and understanding, enabling him to gain insights and acquire wisdom. However, human knowledge is limited and imperfect. In contrast, God possesses complete and perfect knowledge of all things past, present, and future. His omniscience allows Him to have a comprehensive understanding of everything.

Man is moral, but God is morally perfect. Man has been given a moral compass and the ability to discern right from wrong. However, human morality is flawed and subject to personal biases and weaknesses. In contrast, God's moral perfection is beyond reproach. He embodies absolute righteousness and goodness in every aspect of His being.

Man is unitarian, while God is multipersonal. Man exists as an individual being, separate from others. While humans have a sense of unity through shared experiences and relationships, each person has their own unique identity. On the other hand, God exists as a Triunebeing—Father, Son, and Holy Spirit—in perfect unity and harmony. This multipersonal nature of God reflects His infinite love and relational nature.

While man bears the likeness and image of God in certain aspects, such as power, knowledge, morality, and unity, it is essential to recognize that these qualities are limited and imperfect in comparison to God's attributes. Man is not identical to God in every aspect but rather reflects certain aspects of His nature. God is greater in every aspect, possessing unlimited power, perfect knowledge, moral perfection, and a multipersonal nature that surpasses human understanding ("The Trinity Explained," 2016).[27]

Old Testament Bible Verse

Numbers 6:24-26

"The LORD bless you, and keep you; The LORD cause His face to shine on you, And be gracious to you; The LORD [emphasis added] lift up His face to you, And give you peace" (NASB).

Numbers 6:24-26 is a beautiful blessing found in the Old Testament. It is a blessing that invokes the benevolent love of God, the Father of mercies and the fountain of all good. The first line, "The LORD bless thee, and keep thee," illustrates the Divine care and protection that God offers to His people. He desires to bless us in every aspect of our lives and protect us from harm.

The second line of the blessing, "The LORD make his face shine upon thee, and be gracious unto thee," speaks of the redeeming and reconciling grace of our Lord Jesus Christ. This line reminds us that God's face shines upon us with favor and grace. Through Jesus Christ, we receive forgiveness for our sins and are reconciled to God. His grace is a gift we do not deserve, yet it is freely given to us.

The final line of the blessing says, "The LORD lift his countenance upon thee, and give thee peace." This line represents the purity, consolation, and joy we receive through the communion of the Holy Spirit. When God lifts His countenance upon us, it signifies His pleasure and favor towards us. Through the Holy Spirit, we experience a deep sense of peace that surpasses all understanding. This peace comes from knowing that we are in the right relationship with God and that He is with us always.

The blessing given to us in Numbers 6:24-26 beautifully encapsulates the love and blessings that God offers to His people. It reminds us of His care and protection, His redeeming grace through Jesus Christ, and the peace gained from communing with the Holy Spirit. This benediction reminds us of God's unfailing love and desire for our well-being. *It is a powerful declaration of God's goodness and a source of comfort, encouragement, and hope for all who receive it.*

Isaiah 48:16

"Come near to Me, listen to this: From the beginning I have not spoken in secret, From the time it took place, I was there. And now the LORD GOD has sent Me, and His Spirit" (NASB).

In Isaiah 48:16, we witness a conversation between God and LORD YHVH. The context makes it clear that God is speaking here. He declares that He has not spoken in secret from the beginning and has been present throughout all events.

However, the revelation that God is sending LORD YHVH and His Spirit stands out in this verse. This statement implies a plurality within God, with LORD YHVH (the Father) sending both YHVH (His Word) and His Spirit (The Holy Spirit).

This verse highlights a grammatical distinction that suggests the presence of multiple Divine Entities communicating with one another. The use of pronouns such as "Me," "I," and "His" indicates that there are at least two distinct Entities involved in the conversation. God is speaking and referring to sending His LORD YHVH and His Spirit. This linguistic construction establishes a plurality within God.

Genesis 19:24

"Then the LORD rained upon Sodom and upon Gomorrah brimstone and fire from the LORD out of heaven" (KJV).

The book of Genesis, chapter 19, verse 24, says, "And LORD [Jesus] rained on Sodom and Gomorrah brimstone and fire from the LORD [Father] {clarifications added} out of heaven." This verse depicts a significant event in biblical history: Divine intervention destroyed the cities of Sodom and Gomorrah. The context of this event can be traced back to Genesis 18, where YHVH (Jesus) appears to Abraham in human form, shares a meal with him, and engages in a conversation.

In Genesis 18, YHVH visits Abraham, and two other men later revealed to be angels. This visitation is pivotal in Abraham's life, as he is told that his wife Sarah will bear him a son despite their old age. During their interaction, YHVH (Jesus) reveals His plan to investigate the outcry against Sodom and Gomorrah due to their inhabitants' wickedness.

After this conversation with Abraham, YHVH (Jesus) proceeds towards Sodom and Gomorrah. The cities were notorious for their immoral behavior and disregard for ethical principles. Their inhabitants had become deeply entrenched in acts of sin, causing great distress among the righteous people living there. YHVH (Jesus) intended to determine the extent of their wickedness and execute judgment from YHVH (Father).

Zechariah 3:1-2

"Next I saw Joshua the high priest standing before the angel of the LORD, with Satan standing at his right hand to accuse him. The LORD said to Satan, "May the LORD rebuke you, Satan! "May the LORD, who has chosen Jerusalem, rebuke you! Isn't this man like a burning stick snatched from the fire?" (NET).

Zechariah 3:1-2, we witness an interesting dialogue between YHVH, Satan, and Joshua, the high priest. The angel of YHVH presents Joshua before YHVH, with Satan standing at His right hand to accuse him. However, instead of directly rebuking Satan, YHVH says, "YHVH rebuke you, Satan! Indeed, YHVH, who has chosen Jerusalem, rebuke you!" This use of the third Person by YHVH implies that God is more than one Person. It suggests the existence of a Divine Trinity.

By referring to Himself as YHVH, YHVH differentiates Himself from the angel of YHVH and leaves it to YHVH to rebuke Satan. This distinction within the Divine identity supports the concept of the Trinity in theology. *This passage from Zechariah suggests that YHVH is not only referring to Himself as YHVH but also acknowledging another Person within the Divine identity capable of rebuking Satan.* The Book of Jude tells us that only YHVH can rebuke Satan and that if anyone else tries to rebuke Satan, it is blasphemy.[28] Therefore, this YHVH is God also, or He committed a blasphemy statement.

Furthermore, YHVH's statement, "May the LORD, who has chosen Jerusalem, rebuke you! Isn't this man like a burning stick snatched from the fire?" emphasizes the role of YHVH in choosing Jerusalem and delivering it from destruction. This language aligns with the concept of God the Father as the initiator and overseer of salvation. The reference to Jerusalem as a "brand delivered from the fire" symbolizes its redemption and restoration, which reflects the work of Jesus on the cross, saving His people.

Isaiah 44:6

"Thus says the LORD, the King of Israel and his Redeemer, the LORD [emphasis added] of hosts: "I am the first and I am the last; besides me there is no god" (ESV).

Isaiah 44:6, where the LORD, the King of Israel and His Redeemer, declares Himself the first and the last, stating that there is no other god besides Him. This verse is significant as it highlights two Divine beings being called by the Holy Name YHVH, associated with God in the Bible. The mention of two Divine beings being addressed with the same Holy Name raises questions about the nature of God and how it relates to the concept of the Trinity.

Isaiah 44:6 states, "I am the first, and I am the last," a proclamation that echoes throughout the book of Revelation, where Jesus is referred to as the first and the last. This statement serves as a powerful confirmation that Jesus is being called God. In Revelation, Jesus is portrayed as the eternal and all-powerful figure who existed before all things and will exist after all things. The title "First and

Last" emphasizes Jesus' Divine nature and infinite existence, indicating that He is not simply a human prophet or teacher but the embodiment of God Himself. This declaration highlights the unique and Divine status of Jesus in Christian theology.

Therefore, the declaration that the LORD is the first and the last emphasizes His eternal nature. Being the first implies that He has existed since the beginning of time while being the last suggests that He will be present until the end. This statement reinforces the idea of God's omnipresence and eternal existence, further establishing His Divinity.

"Besides me there is no god" is profound here. The Hebrew word "god" is elohim, plural. God of gods, the LORD of Lords, is clearly saying there is no Triune God other than Himself. We need to ensure that this type of content is included in the translations.

Furthermore, the verse addresses the LORD as the King of Israel and His Redeemer. This suggests that two Divine Entities are being referred to here, both of whom are called by the Holy Name YHVH. "King of Israel" implies a ruling authority, while "Redeemer" suggests a role of salvation or deliverance. These two aspects highlight different attributes of God, showcasing His sovereignty and ability to redeem and save His people. It is irrational to think salvation can be found anywhere else other than God. This is literally saying God is all-powerful and all-knowing but cannot save His people, that He had to create a being that is powerful enough to save. This would be giving His Glory to the created being, and this is something which God says He will not do.[29]

Judges

When Samson's birth is foretold to his parents, the Scripture provides us with a vivid account of the Angel or Messenger of the LORD visiting Sampson's mother to deliver instructions on how to raise the boy once he enters the world. This Divine encounter was of great significance, as it set the stage for the remarkable life that Samson would lead. After this encounter, Manoah, Sampson's father, fervently prayed and implored that the man of God be sent back to further clarify these instructions. His desire for a clearer understanding of the Divine guidance bestowed upon them was evident in his plea.

The messenger returned to converse with him in response to Manoah's prayer. Curious and seeking knowledge, Manoah posed a question that had been weighing on his mind: "What is thy name?" In a mysterious and enigmatic manner, the messenger replied, *"Why askest thou thus after my name, seeing it is a secret?"* This cryptic response only added to the intrigue and mystique surrounding this celestial being.

As Manoah offered a meat offering to the LORD, an extraordinary event unfolded before their eyes. The messenger performed a wondrous act, ascending in the altar's flame. Overwhelmed by this awe-inspiring spectacle, Manoah exclaimed, *"We shall surely die because we have seen God."* The magnitude of this encounter left them in awe as they realized the profound nature of their interaction: the Angel of the LORD with Whom they had been conversing had actually been God Himself.

This account of Samson's parents seeking clarity and the subsequent encounter with the messenger raises an interesting point. In his writings, it is plausible that Augur, when he wrote Proverbs 30, delved into the significance of the name of God's son due to the recurring instances in the Old Testament where Yahweh is described as appearing in human form. In these instances, when asked about his name, Yahweh refuses to answer. However, it is essential to note that we, as believers, know the name of God's son - Jesus, also known as Yeshua. The pronunciation may vary, but the essence remains the same. Jesus, as the second Person of the Trinity, is intricately woven into the fabric of the Old Testament.

Proverbs 30:4-6

"Who has gone up to heaven and come down?
Whose hands have gathered up the wind?
Who has wrapped up the waters in a cloak?
Who has established all the ends of the earth?
What is his name, and what is the name of his son?
Surely you know!
"Every word of God is flawless;
he is a shield to those who take refuge in him.
Do not add to his words,
or he will rebuke you and prove you a liar" (NIV).

The concept of God appearing in human form is further reinforced by the understanding that no mortal can witness the glory of God the Father and survive. Therefore, in every instance in Scripture where a human sees God, it can be inferred that they are beholding Jesus. This notion is echoed in John 1:18, which states, "No man hath seen God at any time; the only begotten Son, which is in the bosom of the Father, he hath declared him." Additionally, Hebrews 1 emphasizes that Jesus Christ is the express image of God, signifying that for a mortal to witness God and continue living, they must have encountered the manifestation of God in human form - the Son of God.

Samson's birth and the subsequent interactions with the Messenger of the LORD provide us with a glimpse into the Divine mysteries and the profound nature of God's presence in human form. The significance of the name of God's son, Jesus, is deeply rooted in the Old Testament, where Yahweh's appearances in human form offer a glimpse into the Divine plan and the revelation of God's true nature.

Genesis 48:15-16

"And he blessed Joseph and said, "The God before whom my fathers Abraham and Isaac walked, the God who has been my shepherd all my life long to this day, the angel who has redeemed me from all evil, bless the boys; and in them let my name be carried on, and the name of my fathers Abraham and Isaac; and let them grow into a multitude in the midst of the earth." (ESV)

In this passage, Jacob blesses his son Joseph and mentions three distinct Entities to which he attributes specific characteristics. Firstly, he acknowledges "the God before whom my fathers Abraham and Isaac walked." This refers to the God of their ancestors, implying the continuity of their faith and the presence of a Divine figure throughout their lineage. Secondly, Jacob mentions "the God who has been my shepherd all my life long to this day." Here, he recognizes a personal relationship with God as his shepherd, highlighting the role of God as a caregiver and guide in his life. Lastly, he refers to "the Angel who has redeemed me from all evil." This angel is seen as a redeemer who has saved Jacob from harm and protected him from evil forces.

By mentioning these three Entities in his blessing, Jacob implies the existence of three distinct Persons within the Godhead. The first Entity represents God the Father, whom Abraham and Isaac worshipped and followed. The second Entity represents God the Son, who has shepherded Jacob throughout his life. The third Entity represents God, the Holy Spirit, who is seen as an angelic figure who delivers redemption and protection. This trinitarian understanding aligns with later revelations in the New Testament, where Jesus Christ is identified as the Son of God and the Holy Spirit is recognized as a separate Person within the Triune God.

Furthermore, Jacob's blessing includes a request for these three Entities to bless Joseph's sons, Ephraim and Manasseh, which implies that they have the same power in their Divine blessing. He asks that they carry on his name and the names of Abraham and Isaac, signifying a continuation of their legacy and faith. This demonstrates the importance of passing down God's worship from generation to generation. It also suggests that the blessings and protection of these three Entities are not limited to Jacob alone but are meant to extend to his descendants.

Overall, Genesis 48:15-16 is a trinitarian verse acknowledging the presence and involvement of three distinct Persons within the Godhead. It highlights the role of God the Father, God the Son, and God the Holy Spirit in the lives of believers and emphasizes the continuity of faith throughout generations. This passage provides early evidence for the concept of the Trinity in the Bible and lays the foundation for further understanding of God's Triune Nature in later biblical texts.

YHVH Seen

The concept of God being holy[30] and pure is a fundamental belief in Christianity. The Bible repeatedly emphasizes God's holiness and inability to look upon sin. In the book of Habakkuk, it is written, "Your eyes are too pure to look on evil; you cannot tolerate wrongdoing".[31] This verse highlights the purity and holiness of God, stating that His eyes cannot even bear witness to evil. Similarly, in the book of Isaiah, it is said, "Fear thou not; for I am with thee: be not dismayed; for I am thy God: I will strengthen thee; yea, I will help thee; yea, I will uphold thee with the right hand of my righteousness".[32] These verses illustrate the nature of God as being wholly removed from sin and unrighteousness.

The Bible also teaches that only Jesus has seen the Father.[33] In the New Testament, Jesus Himself states, "No man hath seen God at any time; the only begotten Son, which is in the bosom of the Father, he hath declared him".[34] This verse confirms that no human being has ever seen God except for Jesus, who is both fully human and fully Divine. This further emphasizes the uniqueness and exclusivity of Jesus as the only one who has had direct communion with the Father.[35]

Here is a list of ten Old Testament Bible verses from the King James Bible where YHVH showed up. How is this possible if the Old Testament tells us YHVH cannot look upon sin; all humans are sinful, and Jesus in the New Testament says only He has seen the Father? There is only one mediator between heaven and earth: the Man Christ Jesus. In the Old Testament, the appearance of God is what theologians call a Christophany, which is an Old Testament appearance of Jesus.

If one did not know that God is Triune, one would have to do word gymnastics to show God really did not mean it when He said that He could not look upon sin. One would be diving off a cliff if they were to start this search in an hermeneutics Bible study. They would then have to begin to question everything written, saying, "Did God really mean...."[36] This is just the kind of crafty and cunning language that Satan wants someone to believe. "Ye did God say?"

God is not a God of confusion; He is a God of order[37] and says what He means and means what He says. Lastly, if someone does not know God the Father cannot look upon sin, then they will not grasp the meaning when Jesus on the cross uttered, "Eli, Eli, lema sabachthani," which translated into English means, "My God, My God, why have you forsaken me?"[38] For all eternity, God the Father had to look away from Jesus because Jesus bore every sin on that cross!

1. Genesis 3:8 - "And they heard the voice of the LORD God walking in the garden in the cool of the day: and Adam and his wife hid themselves from the presence of the LORD God amongst the trees of the garden."

1. Genesis 18:1 - "And the LORD appeared unto him in the plains of Mamre: and he sat in the tent door in the heat of the day."

1. Genesis 32:30 - "And Jacob called the name of the place Peniel: for I have seen God face to face, and my life is preserved."

1. Exodus 33:11 - "And the LORD spake unto Moses face to face, as a man speaketh unto his friend."

1. Exodus 33:9 - "And it came to pass, as Moses entered into the tabernacle, the cloudy pillar descended, and stood at the door of the tabernacle, and the LORD talked with Moses."

1. Deuteronomy 5:4 - "The LORD talked with you face to face in the mount out of the midst of the fire."

1. Daniel 7:9 - "I beheld till the thrones were cast down, and the Ancient of days did sit, whose garment was white as snow, and the hair of his head like the pure wool: his throne was like the fiery flame, and his wheels as burning fire."

1. Exodus 33:11 - "And the LORD spake unto Moses face to face, as a man speaketh unto his friend."

1. Judges 6:22 - "And when Gideon perceived that he was an angel of the LORD, Gideon said, Alas, O LORD God! for because I have seen an angel of the LORD face to face."

1. Judges 13:22 - "And Manoah said unto his wife, We shall

surely die, because we have seen God."

Belief in the word of God is a fundamental aspect of faith for individuals. The Bible is considered the sacred text containing God's teachings and guidance for humanity. However, some question or doubt the truthfulness of the Bible, which can affect their perception of God's integrity. When someone questions the accuracy of the word of God, it may imply that they believe there are errors in the Bible or that God was unable to preserve His word. This skepticism challenges the notion of an all-knowing and trustworthy God, raising doubts about His ability to communicate effectively with His followers.

For believers, it is crucial to always side with God and have faith in His word. The Bible is seen as a Divine revelation inspired by God Himself. It is believed to be infallible, without error, and preserved forever.[39] If one doubts the truthfulness of the Bible, one may also cast doubt on God's integrity and His ability to communicate with humanity. This can create a crisis of faith, as it undermines the foundations of one's beliefs. It would be wise to always side with God. He says what He means and means what He says. When He said He was face to face, walked with someone, or others have seen Him, that is precisely what it means!

However, it is essential to approach these doubts and questions with an open mind and a willingness to seek understanding. It is natural for individuals to have moments of uncertainty or skepticism, and it is through these moments that faith can be strengthened. Engaging in thoughtful exploration and study can deepen one's understanding of the Bible and its teachings. It is also important to remember that faith does not require blind acceptance or a lack of critical thinking. Questioning and seeking answers can lead to a deeper understanding of one's faith and a stronger connection with God. It is through seeking knowledge and experience that one can grow spiritually.

Amos 4:10-11

"I sent a plague among you as in Egypt; I killed your young men with the sword, along with your captured horses, And I made the stench of your camp rise up in your nostrils; Yet you have not returned to Me," declares the LORD. "I overthrew you, as God overthrew Sodom and Gomorrah, And you were like a log snatched from a fire; Yet you have not returned to Me," declares the LORD. (NASB)

In the book of Amos, specifically in Amos 4:10-11, there is a passage where the LORD, who is speaking, refers to another being as "God." This "God" is identified as LORD in Genesis 19:24. This particular verse sheds light on the Divine nature of this being and highlights the significance of Their role in the spiritual realm.

Interestingly, in verse 11, the LORD compares His actions to when "God overthrew Sodom and Gomorrah." This comparison implies that another Divine being is at work in these events. Referring to this being as "God" suggests They possess the same power and authority as the LORD Himself.

Hosea 1:6-7

"She conceived again and gave birth to a daughter. Then the LORD said to him, "Name her 'No Pity' (Lo-Ruhamah) because I will no longer have pity on the nation of Israel. For I will certainly not forgive their guilt. But I will have pity on the nation of Judah. I will deliver them by the LORD their God; I will not deliver them by the warrior's bow, by sword, by military victory, by chariot horses, or by chariots." (NET)

In Hosea 1:6-7, the passage begins with "The LORD said to him," indicating that the words spoken are from God the Father.

Verse 7 states, "But I will have compassion on the house of Judah and deliver them by the LORD their God." Here, the reference to "the LORD their God" is most likely a reference to Jesus or the Holy Spirit. This suggests that the deliverance of the house of Judah is accomplished through the work of Jesus or the Holy Spirit. This verse emphasizes the unity of God in His plan for redemption. The unity of God is a foundational belief in Christianity. This unity is evident in Hosea 1:6-7, where both God the Father and Jesus or the Holy Spirit, are involved in the salvation and deliverance of the house of Judah.

Chapter 3: Biblical Foundations of the Trinity New Testament

While some argue that the concept of the Trinity is difficult to find in the Bible, the New Testament provides ample evidence. The problem arises when people begin to doubt or question whether God means what He says in His Word. The most obvious way to see if someone has faith in God's inerrant word is by asking them about John 1:1, which I will break down later in this chapter, which says, "The Word was God." If someone reads this and says, "God doesn't mean the Word is God," there is a good chance this person does not believe God's Word is without error, or worse, that God intentionally uses words to trick people into violating the first commandment.

While some may struggle to accept or understand the Trinity concept, it is essential to remember that God does not play games with His words. He is a God of truth and clarity. The New Testament presents numerous passages that support and affirm the existence of the Trinity. We are responsible as believers to approach these teachings[40] with an open heart and mind, accepting what God has revealed about Himself.

Jesus Baptized

The baptism of Jesus is a pivotal moment in Christian theology, as it signifies the start of His public ministry. According to the Gospel accounts, Jesus was baptized by John the Baptist in the Jordan River. *This act holds immense significance as it represents Jesus' identification with humanity and inaugurates His mission to redeem humanity from their sins.* By participating in this act of baptism, Jesus aligns Himself with humanity and demonstrates His willingness to take on the burdens and struggles of human existence.

What makes Jesus' baptism even more extraordinary is the presence of all three Persons of the Trinity - God the Father, God the Son (Jesus), and God the Holy Spirit. As Jesus emerges from the waters, the heavens open, and the Spirit of God descends upon Him like a dove. At the same time, a voice from heaven declares, "This is my beloved Son, with whom I am well pleased." This remarkable manifestation of the Trinity at Jesus' baptism emphasizes His Divine nature and marks the beginning of His public ministry.

Moreover, Jesus' baptism is unique because He was not baptized into any particular name. While John's baptism was typically associated with repentance and forgiveness of sins, Jesus was sinless and did not require repentance. Instead, His baptism served as a symbolic act, demonstrating His solidarity with humanity and foreshadowing His role as the Savior of humanity. Through this act, Jesus identifies Himself with sinful humanity, paving the way for His ultimate sacrifice on the cross.

The significance of Jesus' baptism extends beyond its immediate context. It has profound implications for Christian theology and for our understanding of salvation. Through His baptism, Jesus models the importance of humility, obedience, and identification with humanity. It serves as a reminder that salvation is not merely a personal experience but also a communal one. Just as Jesus willingly submitted Himself to baptism, Christians are called to follow His example by humbly accepting God's grace and committing to a life of service.

Great Commission

The Bible emphasizes the significance of God's name and word, stating that He holds them above all things. In Psalms 138:2, it is written that God exalts His name and His word, highlighting Their importance in His Divine plan. This verse reminds believers that they should honor and respect God's name and adhere to His word. Additionally, Isaiah 42:8 further reinforces the notion that God does not share His glory. This verse affirms that God alone deserves all the glory and praise and these are not to be shared with any other entity. It emphasizes the uniqueness and sovereignty of God, underlining His position as the supreme being.

In the Christian faith, baptism is a significant and symbolic act performed in adherence to glorify God. It is an outward expression of one's commitment to God and dedication to following His will. Through baptism, individuals publicly declare their faith and affirm their desire to live by God's teachings. By willingly undergoing this sacrament, believers glorify God by acknowledging His authority over their lives and surrendering themselves to His Divine plan. Baptism is a powerful demonstration of obedience and submission, representing a spiritual rebirth and the washing away of sin. Through this act, believers seek to honor and glorify God by aligning their lives with His purpose and inviting His presence to guide and shape their faith journey.

Matthew 28:19, also known as the Great Commission, is a significant passage in the Bible where Jesus instructs His disciples to go and make disciples of all nations, baptizing them in the singular name of the Father, Son, and Holy Spirit. This command implies that these three Entities are equal and worthy of being invoked during baptism. Including all three in this command suggests Their unity and shared Divine nature as part of the one Godhead. It would not make sense for Jesus to include all three if They were not integral parts of the same Divine being.

John 1:1

Daniel B. Wallace is a prominent New Testament scholar known for his expertise in Greek grammar and textual criticism. One of his notable contributions to the field is his analysis of John 1:1, a verse with significant theological implications. In this verse, the author of the Gospel of John writes, "In the beginning was the Word, and the Word was with God, and the Word was God." Wallace's examination of this verse sheds light on its grammatical structure along with the theological concepts it conveys.

Wallace begins by examining the Greek word order of John 1:1, which differs from typical sentence structure. In Greek, the word "logos" (Word) comes first, followed by the verb "ēn" (was), and then the prepositional phrase "pros ton theon" (with God). This unique word order emphasizes the eternal existence of the Word and its close relationship with God. By placing "logos" at the forefront, John highlights its importance as a Divine Entity (Wallace 1996, sec. 1).[41]

Furthermore, Wallace delves into the significance of the phrase "the Word was God." He explains that the Greek construction used here, known as a qualitative predicate nominative, emphasizes the nature, or essence, of the subject rather than equating it with the subject. In other words, John is not saying that the Word is identical to God in personhood, but shares the exact Divine nature. This understanding aligns with Trinitarian theology, which posits that Jesus, as the Word, is entirely God while distinct from God the Father.

Moreover, Wallace explores the implications of the phrase "the Word was with God." The preposition "pros" denotes a face-to-face relationship between two individuals. This context signifies an intimate and personal relationship between the Word and God. This concept suggests that Jesus, as the Word, had a close fellowship with God from eternity past. It also affirms the distinction between Jesus and God, underscoring Their unity and mutual presence.

In addition to analyzing the grammar and syntax of John 1:1, Wallace addresses various textual variants that have arisen throughout history. These variants are differences in wording found in different manuscripts. Wallace meticulously examines these variants and evaluates their impact on understanding the verse. His expertise in textual criticism enables him to weigh the evidence and provide insights into which readings are most likely original.

Overall, Daniel Wallace's extensive analysis of John 1:1 illuminates its grammatical nuances and theological implications. He offers a comprehensive understanding of this pivotal verse by *examining word order, predicate nominatives, prepositional phrases, and textual variants.* His work contributes to a deeper appreciation of the Divinity of Christ as portrayed in John's Gospel and enriches our understanding of Trinitarian theology. Scholars and theologians continue to benefit from Wallace's research on this significant passage in Scripture (Wallace 1996, bk. 1).[42]

John 14:17-23

Jesus speaks to His disciples about the coming of the Holy Spirit and how the Trinity will indwell believers. This passage provides insight into the relationship between God the Father, God the Son, and God the Holy Spirit and how They work together in the lives of believers. Jesus promises that after His departure, He will send the Holy Spirit to be with His followers and to dwell within them. *This indwelling of the Holy Spirit is a manifestation of the Trinity in the lives of believers.*

The passage begins with Jesus stating that the world cannot receive the Holy Spirit because it does not know Him. This suggests a special relationship between the Holy Spirit and those who believe in Jesus. The world, which refers to those who do not have a personal relationship with God, cannot experience this indwelling of the Trinity because they do not have faith in Jesus. However, for those who believe in Jesus, the Holy Spirit comes to dwell within them.

Jesus goes on to explain that when He leaves, He will send another advocate or helper, who is the Holy Spirit. This advocate will be with believers forever and will be in them. Here, Jesus refers to the Trinity coming to indwell believers. The Father sends the Son, and then Jesus sends the Holy Spirit. This shows the unity and cooperation among the members of the Trinity in Their work of redemption.

Think about this, one of the central beliefs of Christianity is that the God of the Bible possesses omniscience, omnipresence, and a unique capability that no other being can claim. According to the teachings of the Bible, God is all-knowing, meaning He has complete knowledge and understanding of everything that has happened, is happening, and will happen in the universe. This Divine attribute sets God apart from others and emphasizes His supreme knowledge and wisdom.

The concept of God's omniscience is deeply rooted in the Bible and is supported by numerous passages. For instance, in the book of Psalms, it is written, "Great is our Lord and mighty in power; his understanding has no limit".[43] This verse highlights the limitless understanding of God, indicating that His knowledge surpasses human comprehension. Similarly, in the New Testament, the apostle John states, "God is greater than our hearts, and he knows everything" (1 John 3:20). This verse further reinforces the belief that only God possesses complete knowledge of everything.

Furthermore, the Bible also teaches that God is omnipresent, meaning that He is present everywhere at all times. This Divine attribute signifies that God is not limited by time or space and can simultaneously be present in every corner of the universe. In the book of Jeremiah, it is written, "Can a man hide in secret places so that I cannot see him? declares the LORD. Do I not fill heaven and earth?" (Jeremiah 23:24). This verse illustrates that no one can escape God's presence because He fills every part of creation.

Luke 1:35

Luke 1:35 is an influential verse highlighting the concept of the Trinity and showcasing the unique actions that each Person of the Trinity - *Father, Son, and Holy Spirit* - can perform. In this verse, the angel Gabriel appears to Mary and announces that she will conceive a child who will be the Son of God. The angel states, "The Holy Spirit will come upon you, and the power of the Most High will overshadow you. So the Holy One to be born will be called the Son of God" (Luke 1:35). This verse portrays the involvement of all three Persons of the Trinity in bringing about this miraculous event.

Firstly, the Holy Spirit is mentioned as the one who will come upon Mary. This action of the Holy Spirit demonstrates His Divine power and presence. Here, His role is to bring about the conception of Jesus in Mary's womb. This action of the Holy Spirit emphasizes His Divine nature and ability to work miracles, which is a unique attribute of God.

Secondly, the power of the Most High is described as overshadowing Mary. The Highest refers to God the Father, often called the Almighty throughout the Bible. The overshadowing of Mary by the power of God signifies His Divine intervention in bringing His Son into the world. This act of intervention demonstrates God's authority and sovereignty over creation. Only God can overshadow and bring about such a miraculous event.

Lastly, the Holy One to be born will be called the Son of God. This refers to Jesus, who is identified as the Son of God throughout the New Testament. The fact that Jesus is referred to as the Son of God indicates His Divine nature and unique relationship with God the Father. This relationship highlights the concept of the Trinity, where Jesus is fully human and Divine. Only God can have a Son who shares His Divine nature.

Luke 1:35 serves as a powerful verse that points out the Trinity and showcases how each Person of the Trinity displays actions that only God can do. The involvement of the Holy Spirit, God the Father, and Jesus in bringing about Jesus' conception emphasizes Their Divine attributes and highlights Their roles in fulfilling God's plan for salvation. This verse serves as a testament to the Triune nature of God and His ability to work miracles through each Person of the Trinity.

The Incarnation

The concept of the Incarnation is a central tenet of Christian theology. It affirms that God took on human form in the Person of Jesus Christ. This profound event is a testament to the love and grace of the Triune God. Each Person of the Trinity—the Father, the Son, and the Holy Spirit—played a vital role in the Incarnation.

Firstly, the Father had a role in the Incarnation, as stated in Hebrews 10:5. This verse highlights God's willingness to send His Son into the world. The Father, out of His deep love for humanity, made the ultimate sacrifice by sending His only begotten Son to dwell among us. This act demonstrates the Father's desire to reconcile humanity with Himself and to offer salvation to all who believe in Jesus Christ. It was through the Father's boundless love that the Incarnation was made possible.

Jesus, as the Son, played an essential role in the Incarnation. Philippians 2:7 describes how Jesus willingly emptied Himself and took on the form of a servant, being born as a human being. In becoming fully human while remaining fully Divine, Jesus demonstrated His humility and obedience to the Father's will. Jesus filled the chasm between God and humanity caused by sin through His incarnation. His life, death, and resurrection brought about salvation and eternal life for all who put their trust in Him.

The Holy Spirit also had a significant role in the Incarnation. Luke 1:35 reveals that it was through the power of the Holy Spirit that Jesus was conceived in the womb of Mary. The Holy Spirit overshadowed Mary, making her the vessel through which God manifested Himself directly into human history. The presence of the Holy Spirit throughout Jesus' life empowered Him to perform miracles, teach with authority, and ultimately offer Himself as a sacrifice for our sins. The Holy Spirit continues to work in believers' lives today, convicting them of sin, empowering them for service, and guiding them in their journey of faith.

The Incarnation is a profound mystery that can be difficult to fully comprehend. However, it is clear that all three Persons of the Trinity—the Father, the Son, and the Holy Spirit—were intimately involved in this Divine act. The Father initiated it out of love for humanity, Jesus willingly embraced it as part of His mission to save us, and the Holy Spirit enabled it by bringing about Jesus' conception. The Incarnation reveals the depth of God's love for us and provides us with hope and salvation. As Christians, we are called to embrace this truth and live in response to God's amazing grace demonstrated through the Incarnation.

The Death of Christ

The death of Christ is a central event in Christian theology, and similarly, all three Persons of the Trinity played a role in it. The Father, as depicted in various scriptures, was involved in the death of Christ. Psalm 22:15 states, "My strength is dried up like a potsherd, and my tongue sticks to my jaws; you lay me in the dust of death." This verse points to the suffering and death that Jesus experienced on the cross, which was part of God's plan for salvation.

Additionally, John 3:16 emphasizes the Father's love for the world, stating that He gave His only Son so that whoever believes in Him shall not perish but have eternal life. *This shows that the Father's will was for Jesus to die for the redemption of humanity.*

Moreover, Romans 8:32 states that God did not spare His own Son but gave Him up for us all. This verse further highlights the Father's role in the death of Christ, as it was His plan and sacrifice for humanity's salvation.

Jesus, as the Son of God, also played a crucial role in His own death. In John 10:18, Jesus declares, "No one takes it from me, but I lay it down of my own accord. I have the authority to lay it down and the authority to take it up again." This verse shows that Jesus willingly chose to lay down His life for the sake of humanity. He had the authority and power to decide when and how He would die.

Furthermore, Galatians 2:20 affirms this self-sacrificial nature of Jesus' death, stating that "I am crucified with Christ: nevertheless I live; yet not I, but Christ liveth in me: and the life which I now live in the flesh I live by the faith of the Son of God, who loved me, and gave himself for me." This verse highlights the fact that Jesus not only died physically but also spiritually, taking on the sins of humanity for himself. In doing so, He made it possible for believers to have a renewed relationship with God.

The Holy Spirit is also involved in the death of Christ. Hebrews 9:14 states, "How much more shall the blood of Christ, who through the eternal Spirit offered himself without spot to God, purge your conscience from dead works to serve the living God?" This verse suggests that it was through the power and guidance of the Holy Spirit that Jesus offered himself as a sacrifice to God. The Holy Spirit enabled Jesus to fulfill His mission on earth and accomplish salvation for humanity. Additionally, throughout Jesus' ministry, He was filled with the Holy Spirit and performed miracles by the power of the Spirit. It was this same Spirit that sustained Him during His crucifixion and resurrection.

All three Persons of the Trinity had a role in the death of Christ. The Father planned and orchestrated the sacrifice, giving His Son for the redemption of humanity. Jesus willingly laid down His life as an act of love and obedience to the Father's will. The Holy Spirit empowered and guided Jesus throughout His ministry and enabled Him to offer Himself as a perfect sacrifice. The death of Christ is a demonstration of the unity and love within the Trinity and serves as the foundation of Christian faith and salvation.

Removing one Person from the Trinity and the death of Christ would not have been possible. For example, if the Holy Spirit had not been present to empower Jesus, He may have struggled to carry out His mission and offer Himself as a sacrifice. Similarly, without the Father's plan and orchestration, there may have been no purpose or direction for Jesus' sacrifice, leading to confusion and a lack of redemption for humanity.

Atonement

Atonement is a central concept in Christian theology, referring to the reconciliation of humanity with God through the sacrificial death of Jesus Christ. It is a complex and profound doctrine highlighting God's love, mercy, and justice. In understanding the Atonement, it is important to recognize the role of the three Persons of the Trinity: God the Father, Jesus the Son, and the Holy Spirit.

In Isaiah 53:6 and 10, we see God the Father's involvement in the Atonement. These verses speak of how "All we like sheep have gone astray; we have turned every one to his own way; and the LORD hath laid on him the iniquity of us all," and how it pleased God to crush Jesus and make His life an offering for sin. This highlights the Divine initiative in bringing about salvation. It was God's plan and will to offer His Son as a sacrifice for sin, demonstrating His love for humanity and His desire to reconcile us to Himself.

Jesus, as the Son of God, played a central role in the atonement. Ephesians 5:2 tells us about those who choose to follow Christ: "And walk in love, as Christ also hath loved us, and hath given himself for us an offering and a sacrifice to God for a sweetsmelling savour." Through His death on the cross, Jesus took upon Himself the sins of humanity, becoming the perfect sacrifice that satisfies the demands of justice and opens the way for forgiveness and reconciliation. Jesus willingly laid down His life out of love for us, demonstrating His obedience to the Father's will.

The Holy Spirit also plays a crucial role in the Atonement. Hebrews 9:14 states that Jesus "How much more shall the blood of Christ, who through the eternal Spirit offered himself without spot to God, purge your conscience from dead works to serve the living God?" The Holy Spirit empowered Jesus to offer Himself as a sacrifice, working through Him to accomplish the work of salvation. The Spirit's role also extends to applying the benefits of Christ's sacrifice to individuals. It is through the work of the Holy Spirit that we are convicted of sin, brought to repentance, and enabled to receive forgiveness and new life in Christ.

These verses and others throughout Scripture highlight how all three Persons of the Trinity are actively involved in the atonement. The Father initiates and plans salvation, the Son offers Himself as a sacrifice; and the Holy Spirit empowers and applies the benefits of Christ's work to individuals. This underscores the unity and cooperation within the Trinity in accomplishing our redemption.

Understanding the role of each Person of the Trinity in the atonement helps us grasp the depth and significance of God's love for us. It reveals His commitment to justice and mercy, as well as His desire to restore our broken relationship with Him. The Atonement reminds us that salvation is not just a one-time event but an ongoing process that involves all three Persons of the Trinity working together for our ultimate reconciliation with God.

Resurrection of Christ

The resurrection of Christ is a foundational belief in Christianity, and it is through this event that believers find hope and assurance of eternal life. The resurrection is a testament to the power and authority of God, and all three Persons of the Trinity—the Father, the Son, and the Holy Spirit – played a crucial role in making it possible.

Firstly, the Father had a significant role in the resurrection of Christ. Acts 2:24 states, "Whom God hath raised up, having loosed the pains of death: because it was not possible that he should be holden of it." This verse emphasizes that God the Father raised Jesus from the dead. Additionally, Romans 6:4 highlights that Jesus was raised from the dead by the glory of the Father. The Father's power and authority were instrumental in bringing about the resurrection, demonstrating His sovereignty over life and death.

Secondly, Jesus the Son also played a vital role in His own resurrection. In John 2:19, Jesus said, "Jesus answered and said unto them, Destroy this temple, and in three days I will raise it up." This statement foreshadows His resurrection, indicating that He had authority over His own life. Furthermore, in John 10:17-18, Jesus declared that He had the power to lay down His life and take it up again. These verses show that Jesus willingly gave up His life on the cross and had the ability to rise from the dead. His resurrection was an act of God's power and a demonstration of His own Divine authority.

Lastly, the Holy Spirit also played a crucial role in the resurrection of Christ. Romans 8:11 states, "But if the Spirit of him that raised up Jesus from the dead dwell in you, he that raised up Christ from the dead shall also quicken your mortal bodies by his Spirit that dwelleth in you." This verse highlights that it was through the power of the Holy Spirit that Jesus was raised from the dead.

Furthermore, 1 Peter 3:18 mentions that Jesus was put to death in the body but made alive by the Spirit. The Holy Spirit's role in the resurrection emphasizes His role as the source of life and His indwelling presence in believers.

Removing one Person from the Trinity would render the resurrection of Christ impossible. The Father's power and authority were necessary to raise Jesus from the dead. Without Him, there would be no resurrection. Similarly, Jesus' authority over His life and willingness to lay it down and take it up again were essential for His resurrection. Without Jesus, there would be no resurrection. The Holy Spirit's power and presence were instrumental in raising Jesus from the dead. Without the Holy Spirit, there would be no resurrection. The Trinity worked together harmoniously to accomplish this miraculous event.

The resurrection of Christ is a pivotal event in Christianity, and all three Persons of the Trinity had a significant role in making it possible. The Father's power and authority, Jesus' own authority over His life, and the Holy Spirit's power and presence all worked together to bring about this miraculous event. Removing any one Person from this equation would render the resurrection impossible. The resurrection of Christ is a testament to the unity and cooperation within the Trinity and serves as a foundation for Christian faith and hope.

Indwelling of Believers

The indwelling of believers is a profound theological concept that highlights the intimate relationship between God and His people. It refers to the presence of the Triune God - Father, Son, and Holy Spirit—dwelling within the hearts of believers. This indwelling is made possible through the work of all three Persons of the Trinity.

Firstly, the role of the Father in the indwelling of believers is evident in Ephesians 4:6, which states that there is "One God and Father of all, who is above all, and through all, and in you all." The Father, as the creator and sustainer of all things, is intimately involved in the spiritual transformation of believers. Through His love and grace, we are adopted into His family and become His children. The indwelling of believers is a result of the Father's desire to have a personal relationship with His people.

Secondly, Jesus, the Son, also plays a significant role in the indwelling of believers. In John 17:26, Jesus prays to the Father, saying, "And I have declared unto them thy name, and will declare it: that the love wherewith thou hast loved me may be in them, and I in them." Through His life, death, and resurrection, Jesus reconciled humanity to God and made it possible for us to be united with Him. The indwelling of believers is made possible through our union with Christ, as stated in Colossians 1:27: "To whom God would make known what is the riches of the glory of this mystery among the Gentiles; which is Christ in you, the hope of glory." Jesus' sacrifice on the cross paved the way for the Holy Spirit to dwell within us.

Lastly, the Holy Spirit is crucial in the indwelling of believers. 1 Corinthians 6:19 says, "What? know ye not that your body is the temple of the Holy Ghost which is in you, which ye have of God, and ye are not your own?" The Holy Spirit is given to believers to seal and guarantee their salvation. He empowers and guides us in our Christian walk, convicts us of sin, and enables us to live a life that pleases God. The indwelling of believers by the Holy Spirit brings about transformation from within, enabling us to live according to God's will.

It is important to note that all three Persons of the Trinity are necessary for the indwelling of believers. If we were to remove one Person from the Trinity, such as Jesus, then His sacrificial death and resurrection would not have taken place. Without Jesus' resurrection, there would be no forgiveness of sins or reconciliation with God. Without Jesus' foundational work, the indwelling of believers would not be possible.

In conclusion, the indwelling of believers is a beautiful aspect of our relationship with God. It demonstrates His desire to dwell within us and transform us into His image. The Father initiates this indwelling through His love and grace. Jesus makes it possible through His sacrificial death and resurrection. The Holy Spirit empowers and guides us in our journey of faith. All three Persons of the Trinity are necessary for the indwelling of believers; without Them, our salvation and transformation would not be possible.

Sanctification of Believers

Sanctification is a crucial aspect of the Christian faith and can be understood as the process by which believers are set apart and made holy. It is a work of God that involves the active participation of all three Persons of the Trinity: the Father, the Son, and the Holy Spirit. As revealed in various biblical passages, each Person of the Trinity plays a unique role in the sanctification of believers.

Jude 1:1 shows that the Father starts the process of sanctification. The passage speaks of believers being "Jude, the servant of Jesus Christ, and brother of James, to them that are sanctified by God the Father, and preserved in Jesus Christ, and called:" The Father's role in sanctification is highlighted as calling and setting believers apart for Christ. It is through the Father's love and keeping that believers are sanctified and preserved.

Jesus the Son, we find in Hebrews 2:11 that He plays a vital role in the sanctification of believers. The verse states, "For both he that sanctifieth and they who are sanctified are all of one: for which cause he is not ashamed to call them brethren." This verse emphasizes that Jesus is both the One who makes people holy and is also united with those who are made holy. Jesus provides the means for believers' sanctification through His sacrificial death on the cross. His perfect obedience and atoning sacrifice make it possible for believers to be set apart and made holy.

The Holy Spirit's role in sanctification is highlighted in 1 Corinthians 6:11, which states, "And such were some of you: but ye are washed, but ye are sanctified, but ye are justified in the name of the Lord Jesus, and by the Spirit of our God." Here, we see that it is through the work of the Holy Spirit that believers are sanctified. The Spirit cleanses and purifies believers, enabling them to be set apart for God's purposes. The Spirit also empowers believers to live holy lives, transforming their hearts and minds to conform to Christ's image.

It is important to recognize that all three Persons of the Trinity are essential for the resurrection of Christ to be possible. If we were to remove one Person from the Trinity, the Divine plan of salvation would be incomplete. The Father's role as the initiator and sustainer of sanctification ensures that believers are set apart for Christ's redemptive work. Jesus' role as the One who makes people holy and is united with them through His incarnation and sacrifice guarantees their sanctification. Finally, the Holy Spirit's work in cleansing, empowering, and transforming believers enables them to fully participate in their sanctification.

The sanctification of believers is a multifaceted process that involves the active participation of all three Persons of the Trinity. The Father initiates and sustains sanctification, Jesus provides the means for sanctification through His sacrificial death and resurrection, and the Holy Spirit empowers and transforms believers for holy living. Their collective work ensures that believers are set apart and made holy. Removing one Person from the Trinity would undermine the Divine plan of salvation and render Christ's resurrection impossible.

Eternal Security of the Believer

The concept of the eternal security of the believer is a fundamental belief in Christianity. It is the belief that once a person has accepted Jesus Christ as their Savior, they are eternally secure in their salvation and cannot lose it. This assurance is supported by various passages in the Bible, including John 10:29, where Jesus says, "My Father, who has given them to me, is greater than all; no one can snatch them out of my Father's hand." This verse emphasizes the role of the Father in securing the believer's eternal salvation.

In addition to the Father's role, Jesus the Son also plays a crucial part in ensuring the eternal security of believers. John 10:28 states, "And I give unto them eternal life; and they shall never perish, neither shall any man pluck them out of my hand." Here, Jesus affirms that He gives believers eternal life, and no external force can separate them from Him. Furthermore, in Romans 8:34, it is stated that Jesus intercedes for believers at the right hand of God. This intercession serves as a constant reminder that Jesus is actively involved in preserving the believer's eternal security.

The Holy Spirit, the third Person of the Trinity, also plays a significant role in ensuring the eternal security of believers. Ephesians 4:30 states, "And grieve not the holy Spirit of God, whereby ye are sealed unto the day of redemption." The sealing of the Holy Spirit signifies that believers are marked as God's own and are protected until the day of redemption. The presence and work of the Holy Spirit within believers provide comfort and assurance of their eternal security.

Each Person of the Trinity has a unique role in securing the eternal salvation of believers. The Father's act of giving believers to Jesus provides a secure foundation for their salvation. Jesus' sacrifice on the cross and His ongoing intercession ensure that believers are eternally secure in Him. The Holy Spirit's sealing guarantees their protection until the final day of redemption.

If one Person were to be removed from the Trinity, particularly Jesus the Son, the resurrection of Christ would not be possible. The resurrection is a pivotal event in Christianity, as it demonstrates Christ's victory over sin and death. Without His resurrection, there would be no hope for eternal life and no assurance of salvation for believers. Furthermore, Jesus' role as our advocate and mediator would be nullified, leaving believers without someone to intercede on their behalf before God.

Scripture supports a fundamental belief in Christianity: *the believer's eternal security.* The Father's role in giving believers to Jesus, Jesus' sacrifice and intercession, and the Holy Spirit's sealing all contribute to this assurance. The removal of any Person from the Trinity would have significant implications for the believer's eternal security, particularly regarding the resurrection of Christ and His ongoing intercession on our behalf.

Who sent the Holy Spirit

In the Book of John, two verses, John 14:26 and John 15:26, seem to contradict each other regarding the sending of the Holy Spirit. However, upon closer examination, it becomes evident that these verses do not contradict each other but rather emphasize the unity of the Father and the Son as one God.

In John 14:26, Jesus tells His disciples about the coming of the Helper, the Holy Spirit, whom the Father will send in Jesus' name. This statement clearly indicates that the Father is doing the sending. Using the term "in Jesus' name" signifies that the Holy Spirit's mission and authority align with Jesus' teachings and purpose. It highlights the intimate connection between the Father and the Son and their cooperative role in sending the Holy Spirit.

On the other hand, John 15:26 presents a slightly different perspective. Here, Jesus states that when the Comforter comes, whom He will send to His disciples from the Father, it is referred to as the Spirit of truth. This statement emphasizes Jesus' role in sending the Holy Spirit. However, it is crucial to note that Jesus is not acting independently of the Father in this action. Rather, His sending of the Holy Spirit is in accordance with the Father's will and purpose.

So, how do we reconcile these seemingly conflicting statements? The key lies in understanding the concept of the Trinity and the nature of God. The Father, Son, and Holy Spirit are distinct Persons within the Godhead but are also one in essence. They operate in perfect unity and harmony. Therefore, when one Person of the Trinity sends another, it is not an act of separation or division but rather an expression of their united purpose and mission.

Both statements in John 14:26 and John 15:26 are true because they highlight different aspects of the sending of the Holy Spirit while affirming God's unity and oneness. The Father is indeed sending the Holy Spirit in Jesus' name, demonstrating their shared authority and purpose. At the same time, Jesus also plays a role in sending the Holy Spirit from the Father, illustrating their cooperative relationship within the Trinity. The Father, Son, and Holy Spirit are distinct yet inseparable, working together in perfect unity for our salvation and spiritual growth.

Chapter 4: Understanding God the Father

84

Agape

God is the same yesterday, today, and forever. This means that God's character and nature are unchanging. He has always been and will always be the same. This idea is rooted in the belief that God is eternal and exists outside of time. It also speaks to the consistency and reliability of God's love, mercy, and faithfulness towards humanity.

However, if God was just one Person for all eternity, the question arises: who was He loving? If there was no one else to love, then love could not be a part of His nature. Love, by its very nature, requires an object to be directed towards. Without someone or something to love, God's capacity for love would be empty and unfulfilled.

Love must be a necessary result of God's creation in order for it to exist within God's Nature. Is the existence of love within God's essence an essential consequence of God's creation? What did God have to create for His love to exist? God would not have had to create anything, since He always was as He is now, Triune, and had always been love itself all along.

If God had to create something to love that would mean He had a need He could not meet, and so the Trinity, which has always been there, appropriately explains how God Loves without having to have created anything. The Trinity enables us to comprehend the impeccable love that emanates from God and which is the source of His love from the beginning of time itself. Since we know God is love, the Trinity helps us understand the perfect love that flows from God.

In Matthew 2:17, we read about the Father's love for His Son, Jesus. This verse highlights the deep affection and care that God has for Jesus. The Greek word used here to describe Jesus is ἀγαπητός (agapetos), which carries a profound meaning. This word is derived from the root word ἀγάπη (agape), which is often used in the New

Testament to depict God's unconditional and selfless love for humanity.

The use of ἀγαπητός in reference to Jesus emphasizes the special bond and endearment between the Father and the Son. It illustrates their intimate relationship, rooted in a love that surpasses all human understanding. This term conveys a sense of affection and denotes the Son's beloved and chosen status. It signifies that Jesus is highly esteemed, revered, and cherished by the Father.

As we delve deeper into the meaning of ἀγαπητός, it becomes evident that it encompasses more than just a sentimental fondness. It implies a Divine purpose and a unique role that Jesus fulfills in God's plan of salvation. This term reinforces the idea that Jesus is not merely loved by the Father, but He is also set apart as the One who brings redemption, reconciliation, and eternal life to all who believe in Him. Did God the Father become ἀγαπητός or has He always been love?

Furthermore, this understanding of God's Nature as unchanging and eternal also has implications for our own understanding of love. If we are made in God's image and likeness, then our capacity for love is also rooted in the act of creation. We are called to love others because a loving God has created us. God's capacity for love would be empty and unfulfilled without someone or something to love.

Lastly, in the final moments of His earthly ministry, Jesus expresses a profound truth in John 17:24. He declares that God the Father loved Him even before the creation of the world. This statement reveals the eternal nature of God's love for Jesus, highlighting the depth and significance of their relationship. It underscores the Divine plan and purpose that were in motion long before humanity came into existence. This verse offers a glimpse into the timeless bond between the Father and the Son, emphasizing the Divine love that transcends time and space. It serves as a reminder of the unbreakable connection between God and Jesus and the profound implications of this love for all those who believe in Him.

Father

The idea that God has a paternal relationship with Jesus is central to understanding the nature of the Holy Trinity. It is important to note that God did not become a father to Jesus at a specific point in time but has always been a father to Him. This emphasizes the unchanging and eternal nature of God within the Trinity.

In the Bible, Jesus often referred to God as His Father. This relationship was not established or created; rather, it has always existed. It is an intrinsic part of their Divine nature. This understanding is supported by various passages in the New Testament, such as John 1:1-2, which states, "In the beginning was the Word, and the Word was with God, and the Word was God. He was with God in the beginning." This passage highlights the eternal existence of Jesus alongside God the Father. God's unchanging and eternal Nature as a father to Jesus reflects the stability and constancy within the Holy Trinity.

Eternal Existence

In Psalm 90:2, it is stated that God the Father is an Eternal Existence. The verse says, "Before the mountains were brought forth, or ever thou hadst formed the earth and the world, even from everlasting to everlasting, thou art God." This verse emphasizes the timeless Nature of God, highlighting His Eternal Existence that spans beyond the creation of the world. This attribute of God being Eternal is found in Psalm 90:2 and can also be observed in various other verses throughout the Bible.

In Isaiah 57:15, it is written, "For thus saith the high and lofty One that inhabiteth eternity, whose name is Holy; I dwell in the high and holy place, with him also that is of a contrite and humble spirit, to revive the spirit of the humble, and to revive the heart of the contrite ones." This verse emphasizes that God lives forever, further emphasizing His Everlasting Nature.

Another example of God's Eternal Nature can be seen in the story of Moses and the burning bush, where God reveals Himself as the "I AM" to convey His timeless Existence. This revelation of God as "I AM" highlights His Eternal Presence and Existence outside time. It is a powerful reminder that God has always Existed and will continue to Exist for eternity. The concept of God's Eternal Nature brings comfort and assurance to believers, knowing that their God is unchanging and constant throughout all of time. It also serves as a reminder of the limitations of human understanding, as we cannot fully grasp the infinite nature of God's Existence. We can only catch glimpses of His Eternal Glory and Majesty.

Holiness

God the Father is described as holy in the Bible, emphasizing His pure and perfect Nature. The concept of holiness signifies His absolute moral perfection and separateness from sin and evil. One of the key passages that highlights the holiness of God the Father is found in the book of Leviticus. In Leviticus 11:44-45, God instructs the Israelites, saying, "For I am the LORD your God: ye shall therefore sanctify yourselves, and ye shall be holy; for I am holy: neither shall ye defile yourselves with any manner of creeping thing that creepeth upon the earth. For I am the LORD that bringeth you up out of the land of Egypt, to be your God: ye shall therefore be holy, for I am holy." This passage reveals that God's Holiness is a standard His people are called to aspire to. It emphasizes His moral purity and sets Him apart from all impurity and sin.

Psalm 99:9 says, "Exalt the LORD our God, and worship at his holy hill; for the LORD our God is holy." This verse calls for reverence and worship of God because of His holiness. It reminds us that we should approach Him with awe and respect, recognizing His perfect and untainted Nature. The book of Proverbs 1:7 states, "The fear of the LORD is the beginning of knowledge: but fools despise wisdom and instruction." Here, the fear of the LORD refers to a deep reverence and awe for God's Holiness. It acknowledges that true wisdom starts with recognizing and honoring Him as Holy.

Omnipotent (All powerful)

In 1 Peter 1:5, the apostle Peter refers to God the Father as omnipotent when he writes, "Who are kept by the power of God through faith unto salvation ready to be revealed in the last time." This verse highlights the belief that God's power is infinite and that it is through this power that believers are kept secure in their faith. The term "omnipotent" signifies God's ability to create and control the universe and His ability to protect and preserve His people.

The idea of God's omnipotence can be found in other verses throughout the Bible. For example, in Jeremiah 32:17, the prophet declares, "Ah LORD God! behold, thou hast made the heaven and the earth by thy great power and stretched out arm, and there is nothing too hard for thee:" This verse emphasizes that God's power extends beyond the limitations of human understanding and capabilities. It affirms that He has complete control over all aspects of creation and can accomplish anything according to His will.

Another verse that speaks to God's omnipotence is found in Matthew 19:26, where Jesus says, "But Jesus beheld them, and said unto them, With men this is impossible; but with God all things are possible." This statement by Jesus reinforces the belief that nothing is beyond God's Power and that He can achieve the seemingly impossible. It serves as a reminder of the limitless nature of His abilities and encourages believers to place their trust in Him.

Omniscience (All knowing)

Omniscience, or the attribute of being all-knowing, is a fundamental aspect of God the Father's character as depicted in the Bible. Jeremiah 17:10 is one of the verses that highlights this attribute, stating, "the LORD search the heart, I try the reins, even to give every man according to his ways, and according to the fruit of his doings." This verse emphasizes that God has complete knowledge and understanding of every individual's thoughts, intentions, and actions. It affirms that God is not only aware of external behaviors but also perceives the innermost motives and desires of every human being.

Throughout the Bible, there are numerous other verses that further support the concept of God the Father's omniscience. For instance, Psalm 139:2-4 states, "Thou knowest my downsitting and mine uprising, thou understandest my thought afar off. Thou compassest my path and my lying down, and art acquainted with all my ways. For there is not a word in my tongue, but, lo, O LORD, thou knowest it altogether." This passage beautifully illustrates God's ability to have complete knowledge of an individual's actions and thoughts even before they occur. It demonstrates that God's knowledge is not limited by time or space but extends beyond human comprehension.

Proverbs 15:3 also emphasizes God the Father's omniscience, stating, "The eyes of the LORD are in every place, beholding the evil and the good." This verse portrays God as constantly vigilant, observing every situation and individual. It conveys that nothing can escape His sight or understanding. This attribute of omniscience provides believers with comfort and reassurance in knowing that God is aware of every circumstance they face and every decision they make.

God's omniscience is not limited to the present moment but also encompasses the past and future. Isaiah 46:10 declares, "Declaring the end from the beginning, and from ancient times the things that are not yet done, saying, My counsel shall stand, and I will do all my pleasure:" This verse highlights God's ability to foresee and comprehend all events throughout history. It reveals His sovereignty and authority over time and affirms that His plans will ultimately prevail.

In conclusion, the Bible consistently portrays God the Father as being omniscient, possessing complete knowledge of all things. Jeremiah 17:10 and other verses highlight this attribute, emphasizing that God not only knows our actions but also understands our thoughts, motives, and desires. The concept of God's omniscience provides believers with comfort, knowing that He sees and comprehends every aspect of their lives. It also affirms His sovereignty over time, as He knows the past, present, and future. Recognizing God as all-knowing allows individuals to trust in His wisdom and guidance in every aspect of their lives.

Omnipresence (All present)

The concept of omnipresence, or being all present, is a fundamental aspect of the nature of God the Father. This attribute is described in Jeremiah 23:24, which states, "Can any hide himself in secret places that I shall not see him? saith the LORD. Do not I fill heaven and earth? saith the LORD." This verse emphasizes that God is not confined to any specific physical location but rather exists everywhere at all times. This understanding of God's omnipresence is further reinforced throughout the Bible.

Furthermore, the book of Proverbs also speaks of God's omnipresence. Proverbs 15:3 states, "The eyes of the LORD are in every place, beholding the evil and the good." This verse emphasizes that God is not only present everywhere but also actively observing and aware of all that occurs. It suggests that nothing escapes His attention and that He is constantly vigilant.

The New Testament also affirms the omnipresence of God the Father. In Acts 17:27-28, the apostle Paul addresses the Athenians and proclaims that God is not far from each one of us. He explains that in Him we live, move, and have our being. This passage emphasizes how God's presence sustains our very existence and how closely connected we are to Him.

These verses highlight the omnipresence of God the Father. They depict a God who is not limited by time or space but exists simultaneously in every place. This understanding of God's omnipresence brings comfort and assurance to believers, knowing that He is always with them and watching over them. It also serves as a reminder that we cannot hide from Him or escape His presence. Ultimately, recognizing God's omnipresence leads us to a deeper sense of reverence and awe for His greatness and power.

❖ ❖ ❖

Chapter 5: Exploring the Son, Jesus Christ

Jesus' ontological Deity is often the target of attack because, through this aspect, the saving power of His blood is derived. The belief in Jesus as the Son of God, fully Divine, is central to the Christian faith. This Divine nature gives His sacrifice on the cross its power to save humanity from sin and reconcile them with God. The attacks on Jesus' Deity ontologically aim to undermine the significance of His blood and the redemptive work it accomplished.

Jesus' Deity ontological concept is rooted in the belief that He is not just a mere human being but the incarnation of God Himself. This ontological understanding is essential for comprehending the salvific power of His blood. Through Jesus' Divine nature, His sacrifice becomes efficacious for the salvation of humanity. His blood, shed on the cross, is seen as the ultimate atonement for sin, cleansing and redeeming all who believe in Him.

However, throughout history, there have been various attempts to challenge and attack Jesus' Deity ontologically. These attacks come from different sources, including philosophical, religious, and even secular perspectives. Some argue that Jesus was merely a great moral teacher or a prophet, denying His Divine nature altogether. Others propose alternative theories about His Identity, suggesting that He was just an enlightened individual or a mythological figure.

These attacks on Jesus' Deity ontologically are not new; they have been present since the early days of Christianity. In fact, even during Jesus' earthly ministry, He faced opposition and disbelief regarding His Divine claims. The religious leaders of His time accused Him of blasphemy for proclaiming Himself as the Son of God. This pattern continued in subsequent centuries as various heresies emerged, challenging the orthodox understanding of Jesus' Divinity.

Jesus' Deity is attacked because it is at the core of Christianity's message of salvation. If Jesus is not truly Divine, then His sacrifice loses its redemptive power. The blood shed on the cross becomes meaningless if it does not come from a Divine source. By attacking Jesus' Deity ontologically, critics attempt to undermine the significance of His blood as the means of salvation.

However, despite these attacks, the belief in Jesus' Deity remains a fundamental tenet of Christianity. Through this belief, Christians understand and experience the saving power of His blood. The very essence of Christianity lies in the affirmation that Jesus is both fully human and fully Divine, and it is in this union that salvation is found.

In conclusion, attacks on Jesus' Deity ontologically aim to undermine the saving power of His blood. The belief in Jesus as fully Divine is central to Christianity's understanding of salvation. By attacking His Divinity, critics seek to diminish the significance of His sacrifice on the cross. However, despite these challenges, the belief in Jesus' Deity remains an essential aspect of the Christian faith and plays a crucial role in understanding and experiencing the redemptive power of His blood.

Deceive by Satan

Throughout history, there have been numerous attempts to discredit the Deity of Jesus Christ. It is in Jesus' blood, through His role as Savior, that individuals find salvation. The devil, being aware of this truth, seeks to deceive and mislead people by presenting a counterfeit version of Jesus. If one falls for this deception and places their hope for salvation in a false messiah, their chances of being saved are jeopardized.

Attacks on Jesus' Deity are not a new phenomenon. From the early days of Christianity to the present, skeptics have questioned and challenged the Divinity of Jesus. This is because they understand that if Jesus is Divine, His sacrifice holds ultimate power and significance for humanity's salvation. By attacking Jesus' Deity, critics hope to undermine the very foundation of Christianity and the belief in salvation through Him.

The concept of salvation is central to the Christian faith. Through Jesus as Savior, believers find redemption from their sins and the promise of eternal life. The blood of Jesus shed on the cross is seen as atonement for humanity's sins. This belief is rooted in biblical teachings and has been a cornerstone of Christian theology for centuries.

However, the devil seeks to distort this truth by promoting a fake, made-up version of Jesus. This false messiah may appear to be appealing and persuasive, but ultimately, it cannot save. If someone places their hope for salvation in a counterfeit Jesus, they are placing their trust in a lie. The devil's aim is to lead people away from the true Savior, God Jesus Christ, and ultimately rob them of the opportunity for eternal life.

Recognizing the tactics of the devil is essential for believers. It requires discernment and knowledge of God's Word to differentiate between the true Jesus and the counterfeit versions presented by the enemy. False teachings and distorted beliefs about Jesus can be enticing, but they ultimately lead to spiritual deception.

Eternal Existence

Jesus's eternal existence is fundamental to Christian theology, supported by numerous biblical passages. Micah 5:2 states, "But thou, Bethlehem Ephratah, though thou be little among the thousands of Judah, yet out of thee shall he come forth unto me that is to be ruler in Israel; whose goings forth have been from of old, from everlasting." This verse implies that Jesus' origins are not limited to His earthly birth but rather have existed since ancient times. Similarly, John 1:2 affirms Jesus' eternal existence by saying, "The same was in the beginning with God." This verse establishes that Jesus was present with God at the beginning of creation, emphasizing His Eternal Nature.

The book of Revelation also provides evidence for Jesus' Eternal Existence. Revelation 1:8 states, "I am Alpha and Omega, the beginning and the ending, saith the Lord, which is, and which was, and which is to come, the Almighty." This verse identifies Jesus as the one who is to come and the Almighty, indicating His Divine and timeless Nature. Additionally, Revelation 1:17 describes Jesus as the One Who is alive forever and ever. These verses highlight Jesus' Eternal Existence beyond time and reinforce His Divinity.

Isaiah 41:4 also indirectly supports the concept of Jesus' Eternal Existence by emphasizing God's unique position as the first and the last. This verse states, "Who hath wrought and done it, calling the generations from the beginning? I the LORD, the first, and with the last; I am he." God asserts His Eternal Nature by identifying Himself as both the First and the Last.

Jesus' Eternal Existence provides comfort and assurance to believers. It assures them that their faith is anchored in a timeless and unchanging Savior and offers hope for eternal life for those who trust in Him. The understanding of Jesus' Eternal Existence encourages believers to place their trust in Him and rely on His unfailing love and power.

In his work "Fragments of Clemens Alexandrinus," Clement of Alexandria expounds on the concept of the beginning, explaining that the start of a generation is inseparable from the commencement of the Creator. He delves into the idea that the phrase "that which was from the beginning" refers to the generation without beginning meaning the Son, who exists in Perfect Unity with the Father. The phrase "In the beginning was the Word"[44] emphasizes the Son's Eternal and uncreated Nature even more because He is the Word from the beginning and thus He shares the same substance as the Father (Clement of Alexandria, 1885).[45]

Holiness

Jesus is often referred to as the Holy One in the Bible, emphasizing His Divine Nature and purity. In Acts 3:14, Peter addresses the crowd after healing a lame man, proclaiming, "But ye denied the Holy One and the Just, and desired a murderer to be granted unto you;" This verse clearly identifies Jesus as the Holy One, signifying His perfect righteousness and moral purity. Throughout the New Testament, numerous references further affirm Jesus' Holiness.

In the book of Hebrews 7:26, Jesus is described as being "For such an high priest became us, who is holy, harmless, undefiled, separate from sinners, and made higher than the heavens;" This verse highlights Jesus' complete separation from sin and His Moral Perfection. It underscores the fact that Jesus is not merely a good teacher or a wise prophet but is truly holy in every aspect of his being.

Another verse that emphasizes Jesus' holiness is found in 1 Peter 2:22, which states, "Who did no sin, neither was guile found in his mouth:" This verse emphasizes Jesus' sinlessness and integrity. It speaks to His perfect obedience to God the Father's commandments and His unwavering commitment to truth and righteousness.

Additionally, in 2 Corinthians 5:21, we read, "For he hath made him to be sin for us, who knew no sin; that we might be made the righteousness of God in him." This verse speaks to Jesus' holiness by highlighting His sacrificial role in taking the sins of humanity upon Himself. It portrays Jesus as the spotless Lamb of God who willingly bore our sins on the cross to reconcile us to God.

Furthermore, in John 8:46, Jesus himself declares, "Which of you convinceth me of sin? And if I say the truth, why do ye not believe me?" This statement challenges His opponents to find any fault or wrongdoing in Him. By asking this question, Jesus asserts His own holiness and sets Himself apart from all other human beings.

Lastly, in Revelation 3:7, Jesus is referred to as "he that is holy, he that is true." This title emphasizes Jesus' absolute truthfulness and integrity. It underscores His Divine Nature and highlights His uniqueness among all other beings.

Omnipotent (All powerful)

In 2 Corinthians 12:9, the apostle Paul refers to Jesus as being omnipotent, which means all-powerful. This verse states, "And he said unto me, My grace is sufficient for thee: for my strength is made perfect in weakness. Most gladly therefore will I rather glory in my infirmities, that the power of Christ may rest upon me." Here, Paul recounts an experience where he pleads with God to remove a thorn from his flesh. However, instead of removing the thorn, Jesus tells Paul that His grace is enough and that His power is made perfect in weakness. This verse highlights the concept of Jesus' omnipotence and how He can display His power even in our moments of weakness.

Throughout the Bible, there are numerous verses that speak to the omnipotence of Jesus. For instance, in Matthew 28:18, Jesus says, "And Jesus came and spake unto them, saying, All power is given unto me in heaven and in earth." This statement emphasizes His ultimate power and dominion over all things. Similarly, Colossians 1:16-17 states that "For by him were all things created, that are in heaven, and that are in earth, visible and invisible, whether they be thrones, or dominions, or principalities, or powers: all things were created by him, and for him:." These verses affirm Jesus' role as the Creator and sustainer of the universe, further underscoring His omnipotence.

Another verse that speaks to Jesus' omnipotence is found in John 1:3, which states, "All things were made by him; and without him was not any thing made that was made." This verse asserts that nothing was created without Jesus' involvement. It emphasizes His power to bring into existence everything that exists. Additionally, Hebrews 1:3 proclaims that Jesus is "the radiance of the glory of God and the exact imprint of his nature, and he upholds the universe by the word of his power." This verse highlights Jesus' role in upholding and sustaining all creation through the sheer power of His word.

Furthermore, the miracles performed by Jesus during His earthly ministry serve as a testament to His omnipotence. In Mark 4:35-41, we read about Jesus calming a storm with a simple command. The disciples were terrified as the waves crashed against their boat, but Jesus rebuked the wind and said to the sea, "Peace! Be still!" Instantly, the wind ceased, and there was a great calm. This miraculous event demonstrated Jesus' authority over nature and His ability to exercise complete control even over powerful forces.

Omniscience (All knowing)

As revealed in the Bible, Jesus possesses the attribute of omniscience, which means that He is all-knowing. This is evident in various verses, including Revelation 2:23. In this verse, Jesus declares, "all the churches shall know that I am he which searcheth the reins and hearts: and I will give unto every one of you according to your works." This statement reveals Jesus' knowledge and understanding of individuals' innermost thoughts and intentions. It demonstrates that He has complete knowledge of every person's actions and motivations. When Jesus says, "I am He" in Revelation 2:23, many wonder why does Jesus say this? Jesus is making the connection to His readers by saying that He is also the YHVH in Jeremiah 17:10, which speaks of God the Father. This connection solidifies Jesus' Divinity and authority over all creation.

Throughout the Gospels, we also see instances where Jesus displays His omniscience. For example, in John 1:48, Jesus meets Nathanael and tells him, "Before that Philip called thee, when thou wast under the fig tree, I saw thee." This statement astounds Nathanael because it reveals that Jesus had knowledge of a personal moment of which no one else was present. Similarly, in John 4:16-18, Jesus meets a Samaritan woman at a well and tells her about her past marriages and current relationship status. This revelation surprises the woman and leads her to acknowledge Jesus as a prophet.

In addition to these specific instances, Jesus' overall ministry and teachings also reflect His omniscient nature. He often knew people's thoughts before they even spoke them out loud. In Mark 2:8, when Jesus forgives a paralyzed man's sins, the scribes question His authority. Jesus responds by asking them why are they questioning within their hearts? This shows that Jesus not only has knowledge of their thoughts but is also able to address them directly.

Furthermore, Jesus frequently and quite accurately predicts future events. In Matthew 26:34, Jesus predicts Peter's denial before it happens. He tells Peter that he will deny Him three times before the rooster crows. Later, in Matthew 26:75, this prediction comes true. These prophecies demonstrate Jesus' foreknowledge of events that are yet to occur.

Jesus's omniscience is not limited to His earthly ministry but extends to His Divine nature as well. In Colossians 2:3, it is stated that within Jesus "are hidden all the treasures of wisdom and knowledge." This verse emphasizes that all wisdom and knowledge can be found in Christ alone.

The attribute of omniscience is crucial because it reveals Jesus' Divine Nature and authority. It assures believers that He knows them intimately and understands their deepest thoughts and desires. It also highlights His ability to guide and lead people with perfect knowledge and wisdom.

The Bible clearly portrays Jesus as possessing the attribute of omniscience. Through verses like Revelation 2:23 along with various instances throughout the Gospels, we see that Jesus has complete knowledge of people's thoughts, intentions, past events, and future occurrences. His omniscience is a testament to His Divinity and authority as the Son of God. Believers can find comfort in knowing that Jesus understands them completely and can provide guidance based on His perfect knowledge and wisdom.

Omnipresence (All present)

Omnipresence, the state of being all present, is a concept that is often attributed to God. However, in Matthew 18:20 along with other verses, Jesus also exhibits this quality. In Matthew 18:20, Jesus says, "For where two or three are gathered together in my name, there am I in the midst of them." This statement highlights Jesus' ability to be present wherever His followers gather in His name. It emphasizes His omnipresence, as He promises to be present with His disciples regardless of their physical location.

Throughout the New Testament, there are several instances where Jesus demonstrates His omnipresence. In John 14:23, Jesus says, "Jesus answered and said unto him, If a man love me, he will keep my words: and my Father will love him, and we will come unto him, and make our abode with him." Here, Jesus assures His disciples that both He and the Father will come and make their dwelling with those who love and obey Him. This indicates that physical boundaries do not limit Jesus and that He will be present with believers wherever they may be.

Jesus' omnipresence can be seen in Matthew 28:20, where He says, "Teaching them to observe all things whatsoever I have commanded you: and, lo, I am with you always, even unto the end of the world. Amen." Jesus made this statement after His resurrection and before His ascension into heaven. It shows that Jesus remains present with His disciples through the Holy Spirit even after His physical departure from the earth. This supports the notion that Jesus transcends time and space and is accessible to His followers in all eras.

Granville Sharp Rule

Conjunctions are words that connect words, phrases, and clauses. "And" is a coordinating conjunction, which joins two parts of a sentence. It doesn't qualify or quantify things, but rather, it joins them. For example, in the sentence "Why don't you go upstairs and clean up your room?," the word "and" can be replaced with "then" and the sentence will still remain the same.

The Granville Sharp Rule is a grammatical principle used in biblical interpretation that helps determine the meaning of specific passages in the New Testament. This rule is named after Granville Sharp, an English abolitionist and biblical scholar who formulated this principle in the late 18th century. The rule states that when the conjunction "and" (Greek: kai) connects two nouns of the same case, and the first noun has the definite article (Greek: ho), while the second does not, both nouns refer to the same person or thing. In other words, this rule states that two nouns joined by "and" with one of them having the definite article, refer to the same thing rather than two different people or things.

One example of the Granville Sharp Rule can be found in Titus 2:13, which says, "while we wait for the blessed hope—the appearing of the glory of our great God and Savior, Jesus Christ." The Greek phrase "our great God and Savior" in this verse follows the Granville Sharp Rule's pattern. The phrase consists of two nouns, "God" and "Savior," connected by "and." The first noun, "God," carries the definite article, while the second noun, "Savior," does not. According to the rule, both nouns refer to the same Person, Jesus Christ. *Therefore, this verse affirms Jesus as both God and Savior.*

Another example is 2 Peter 1:1, which states, "Simon Peter, a servant and apostle of Jesus Christ." Here again, we see two nouns connected by "and," with the first noun having the definite article. The Granville Sharp Rule would suggest that Peter refers to himself as a servant and apostle of Jesus Christ, which highlights his role and position in Jesus.

The Granville Sharp Rule can help clarify certain passages in the New Testament where there may be ambiguity or debate about the identity or nature of certain individuals or entities. By understanding and applying this grammatical principle, biblical scholars and interpreters can gain insights into the intended meaning behind these passages.

It is worth noting that while the Granville Sharp Rule provides a helpful guideline for interpreting certain verses, it is not a universal rule that can be applied to every instance of nouns connected by "and." There are exceptions and variations in Greek grammar that also need to be considered. Moreover, translating Greek to English can sometimes introduce complexities requiring additional study and analysis. Nevertheless, understanding and applying principles such as the Granville Sharp Rule can contribute to a more accurate interpretation of biblical texts.

Emmanuel

Matthew 1:23 and Isaiah 7:14 are two biblical passages highlighting the significance of the title "Emmanuel" for Jesus, indicating that He is indeed God. Matthew 1:23 is written, "Behold, a virgin shall be with child, and shall bring forth a son, and they shall call his name Emmanuel, which being interpreted is, God with us." This verse clearly states that Jesus will be known as Emmanuel, which means "God with us." Similarly, Isaiah 7:14 prophecies the coming of a child called Immanuel, signifying that God will be present among His people. These passages affirm that Jesus is not only a human being but also Divine, being God Himself.

The title "Emmanuel" is a masculine name of Hebrew origin that means "God is with us." It's a variant spelling of Immanuel, which is the more accurate transliteration from Hebrew. Emmanuel holds profound theological significance, emphasizing Jesus' Divinity. Naming Him Emmanuel implies that God Himself has come as a man to dwell among His people. This title highlights the unique nature of Jesus' identity and mission. He is not merely a prophet or a teacher, but the embodiment of God's presence on earth. Through Jesus, God reveals Himself to humanity in a tangible and accessible way.

If Emmanuel were not a title for Jesus, it would imply that Mary did not follow God's instructions through the angel Gabriel. In Luke 1:31, the angel tells Mary she will conceive a son named Jesus. However, in Matthew's account, Joseph is instructed to name the child Emmanuel. Understanding that both names are significant in and of themselves will help to explain this apparent discrepancy. "Jesus" signifies His role as the Savior Who will save people from their sins, while "Emmanuel" emphasizes His Divine nature.

Mary's obedience to God's instructions is evident in her willingness to accept her role as the mother of Jesus. She faithfully performed her part in God's plan without hesitation or doubt. While it is true that Mary named her son Jesus in accordance with the angel's instructions, this does not take away from the fact that Jesus is also appropriately known as Emmanuel. The names used in different accounts serve different purposes and emphasize different aspects of Jesus' identity and mission.

Matthew 1:23 and Isaiah 7:14 establish the title "Emmanuel" as significant for Jesus because it highlights His Divinity. The name signifies that Jesus is not simply a human being but God Himself, dwelling among His people. Mary's obedience to God's instructions is evident in her acceptance of her role as the mother of Jesus. The two different names used for Jesus in these different accounts emphasize the multiple aspects of His identity and mission. Thus, "Emmanuel" remains a significant title for Jesus as it affirms His Divine Nature.

Through the course of human history, God has always shown compassion toward mankind; nevertheless, in recent times, His generosity has reached beyond anything that anybody could have conceived of - so much so, that He gave His Son to redeem the world. In Christ, mercy, truth, and life are manifested for sinners, for those straying, and for the dead. Christ unites our humble nature in all circumstances with His Divinity. Thus - the God born of God became a human born of a human (Leo the Great, 1996).[46]

The Rock

In Isaiah 26:4, the LORD declares that in Him there is an "everlasting Rock." This significant statement points to the eternal nature and stability found only in God. The term "Rock" is a metaphor used throughout the Bible to describe God's strength, faithfulness, and dependability. It signifies a solid foundation for building our lives and trust in times of uncertainty.

As we examine the New Testament, we see a clear identification of this "Rock" as Jesus Christ Himself. In 1 Corinthians 10:4, the apostle Paul refers to the Israelites in the wilderness and states, "For they drank from the spiritual Rock that followed them, and the Rock was Christ." Here, Paul draws a parallel between the physical provision of water from a rock in the Old Testament and the spiritual provision of salvation through Jesus in the New Testament. He explicitly states that the Rock was Christ, confirming that Jesus is the everlasting Rock mentioned in Isaiah.

Further evidence of Jesus being identified as the Rock can be found in Matthew 16:18. In this passage, Jesus tells Peter, "And I tell you, you are Peter, and on this rock I will build my church, and the gates of hell shall not prevail against it." Although there is some debate about the interpretation of this verse, many scholars believe that Jesus is referring to Himself as the foundational Rock upon which He will build His church. This interpretation aligns with Isaiah 26:4, emphasizing Jesus' role as the everlasting Rock.

Additionally, Ephesians 2:20 refers to Jesus as the Cornerstone of the church. A cornerstone is a fundamental stone that holds together and aligns an entire building. It provides stability and strength to the structure. In this context, Jesus is seen as the Cornerstone that unifies and supports His church. This concept echoes the idea of an everlasting Rock that offers security and reliability.

Throughout the New Testament, Jesus' Deity and eternal Nature are emphasized. In John 1:1-3, it is stated that "In the beginning was the Word, and the Word was with God, and the Word was God. All things were made by him; and without him was not any thing made that was made." This passage establishes Jesus' preexistence and Divine identity. As such, He can be understood as the everlasting Rock mentioned in Isaiah 26:4.

LORD of lords

Deuteronomy 10:17 refers to the LORD as the "LORD of lords." This title signifies God's supreme authority and sovereignty. The term emphasizes that God is above all earthly rulers and beings. It highlights His unmatched power and dominion over all creation. This verse in Deuteronomy reflects God's awe-inspiring Nature and His position as the ultimate Ruler.

In Acts 10:34, Jesus is identified as the LORD of lords. This passage reveals that Jesus, being the Son of God, shares in the Divine authority and sovereignty. It indicates that Jesus possesses the same attributes and characteristics as the LORD mentioned in Deuteronomy 10:17. This identification highlights the Divinity of Jesus and His role as the ultimate Ruler and authority in the Kingdom of God.

Similarly, in Revelation 17:14 and 19:16, Jesus is referred to as the LORD of lords once again. These verses further affirm that Jesus holds supreme power and authority over all people and things, and emphasize His role as the conqueror and judge of the world. By identifying Jesus as the LORD of lords, these passages reinforce His Divine Nature and position as the New Testament's ultimate Ruler.

It is important to note that these references to Jesus as the LORD of lords do not imply a change in God's Nature. The Bible teaches that God does not change. Malachi 3:6 states, "I am the LORD, I do not change." Therefore, when Deuteronomy 10:17 identifies God as the LORD of lords, it is consistent with the identification of Jesus as the same in Acts and Revelation.

The identification of Jesus as the LORD of lords is significant because it reveals His Divine Nature and His position as the ultimate Ruler over all creation. It highlights His authority and sovereignty in both the Old and New Testaments. This identification also reinforces the concept of God's unchanging Nature, as revealed in

Deuteronomy. It demonstrates the continuity between the Old Testament prophecies with their fulfillment in Jesus in the New Testament.

Whom They Pierced

In Zechariah chapter 12, we witness the powerful words of the LORD Himself speaking through the prophet. The chapter begins with a declaration from the LORD that He will make Jerusalem a cup of trembling for all people and that Judah will be a burdensome stone for all nations. The LORD further states that not only will He make Jerusalem a burdensome stone for all people, but that they will be cut to pieces if they try to lift it. These verses highlight the sovereignty and power of the LORD, demonstrating His authority over all nations.

As we delve deeper into Zechariah chapter 12, we see a remarkable prophecy about the coming of the Messiah. Verse 10 states, "And I will pour upon the house of David, and upon the inhabitants of Jerusalem, the spirit of grace and of supplications: and they shall look upon me whom they have pierced, and they shall mourn for him, as one mourneth for his only son, and shall be in bitterness for him, as one that is in bitterness for his firstborn." This verse is significant as it foretells the piercing of the Messiah and the resulting mourning by the people.

The identification of this pierced figure as Jesus is made clear in the New Testament. In John 19:34-37, we find the fulfillment of Zechariah's prophecy. It describes the crucifixion of Jesus and how one of the soldiers pierced His side with a spear, fulfilling the prophecy of Zechariah 12:10. John explicitly states that these things were done so that "the scripture should be fulfilled, A bone of him shall not be broken. And again another scripture saith, They shall look on him whom they pierced." This connection between Zechariah's prophecy and Jesus' crucifixion solidifies Jesus as the One whom they pierced.

Furthermore, in Revelation 1:7, we see another reference to Zechariah's prophecy regarding Jesus' piercing. The verse states,

"Behold, he cometh with clouds; and every eye shall see him, and they also which pierced him: and all kindreds of the earth shall wail because of him. Even so, Amen." This verse not only confirms Jesus as the One whom they pierced but also emphasizes His second coming along with the universal recognition of His authority.

The identification of Jesus as the LORD who speaks through the prophet in Zechariah chapter 12 is an important aspect of understanding His Divinity and fulfillment of prophecy. It demonstrates His role as the long-awaited Messiah who was pierced for the sins of humanity. Through His sacrifice, Jesus offers redemption and salvation to all who believe in Him. The connection between Zechariah's prophecy and its fulfillment in Jesus further strengthens our faith in Him as the Son of God and our Savior.

LORD Only Saviour

In the Old Testament, there are multiple references to the LORD as the Saviour. One such verse is Isaiah 43:11, which states, "I, even I, am the LORD; and beside me there is no saviour." This verse clearly identifies the LORD as the only Saviour. Additionally, Hosea 13:4 reinforces this idea, proclaiming, "Yet I am the LORD thy God from the land of Egypt, and thou shalt know no god but me: for there is no saviour beside me." These verses emphasize that the LORD is not only the One true God but also the only Saviour.

In Isaiah 45:21-22, we find a compelling passage that further strengthens the connection between the LORD and Jesus. It says, "Tell ye, and bring them near; yea, let them take counsel together: who hath declared this from ancient time? who hath told it from that time? have not I the LORD? and there is no God else beside me; a just God and a Saviour; there is none beside me. Look unto me, and be ye saved, all the ends of the earth: for I am God, and there is none else." Here, the LORD clearly proclaims Himself as not only a just God but also a Saviour. This passage indicates that salvation can only be found in Him.

In the New Testament, we see how Jesus fulfills these prophecies of the LORD as the Saviour. Throughout the Gospels, Jesus consistently demonstrates His authority to save and forgive sins. In Luke 7:48-50, Jesus tells a woman who had shown great love and repentance, "Thy sins are forgiven... Thy faith hath saved thee; go in peace." These words echo the message of salvation proclaimed by the LORD in the Old Testament.

Moreover, it is significant to note that Jesus' name in Hebrew is Yashua, which means "Saviour" or "salvation." This further emphasizes His role as the one who brings salvation to humanity. The Hebrew word for saviour is derived from Yashua's name itself.

Thus, when we refer to Jesus as our Saviour, we are acknowledging His identity as the one who saves.

The identification of Jesus as both the LORD and the Saviour is crucial in understanding His Divinity. In John 8:58, Jesus says to the Jews, "Before Abraham was, I am." By using the phrase "I am," Jesus claims to be the same LORD who spoke to Moses at the burning bush in Exodus 3:14, which states, "And God said unto Moses, I Am That I Am: and he said, Thus shalt thou say unto the children of Israel, I Am hath sent me unto you." This statement solidifies Jesus' Divine Nature and His eternality.

Through these passages and connections, it becomes evident that Jesus is indeed God Himself. He is not merely a prophet or a teacher but the LORD of the Old Testament who came to earth as our Saviour. The LORD's identity as Jesus is supported by biblical evidence and fulfilled prophecies. As believers, we can find assurance and hope knowing that our Saviour is none other than God Himself.

Chapter 6: The Holy Spirit

The Holy Spirit, often misunderstood as merely a force or abstract concept, is a distinct Person within the Trinity, endowed with intelligence, emotions, and will. This Entity isn't an impersonal force but One that engages in teaching, guiding, and comforting, demonstrating personal attributes such as thinking, feeling, and deciding. The Holy Spirit, referred to by various names in Scripture, underscores His integral role in the Christian faith, from creation to guiding believers in truth and moral correctness. His personhood is essential, highlighting not just His power but His active, relational presence in believers' lives.

This chapter aims to navigate the complex yet fascinating theology surrounding the Holy Spirit, focusing on scriptural evidence of His personhood, His attributes, and His undisputed role within the Trinity. By exploring His various titles that underline His Divine nature and contributions, from being called God in Acts 5:3-4, to His involvement in creation and scripture inspiration, readers will gain a deeper understanding of His essence and how to engage meaningfully with Him. Through dissecting the Holy Spirit's characteristics and examining His unity with the Father and the Son, this piece reveals His indispensable role in the believer's life and the broader Christian doctrine.

The Holy Spirit is known by a number of names and titles in the Bible that emphasize His Divine Nature and qualities. In Acts 5:3-4, He is called God, emphasizing His Deity and equality with the Father and Son. This verse reveals that lying to the Holy Spirit is lying to God Himself. Additionally, the Holy Spirit is referred to as the Spirit of God in Genesis 1:2 and Judges 3:10, further emphasizing His role as a part of the Triune God.

Not only is the Holy Spirit called God, but He is also considered God in Acts 28:25–27, 2 Corinthians 6:16, and Hebrews 3:7–9.

These passages show that the Holy Spirit is a Divine being who deserves our worship and reverence. Furthermore, the Holy Spirit is treated as equal to God the Father and Son in numerous biblical references. In Matthew 3:16, for example, we see the Holy Spirit descending on Jesus at His baptism while the Father speaks from heaven. This demonstrates the equal presence and importance of all three Persons of the Trinity.

Hebrews 9:14 highlights the Holy Spirit's Eternal Nature. This verse states that Christ offered Himself through the eternal Spirit, indicating that the Holy Spirit has always existed and is not subject to time or limitations. Similarly, Romans 8:2 describes the Holy Spirit as self-existent, meaning He does not depend on anyone or anything for His existence. This further emphasizes His Divine Nature and independence.

The omnipresence of the Holy Spirit is emphasized in Psalm 139:7–8. These verses state that there is no place where one can escape from the presence of the Spirit. This attribute demonstrates that the Holy Spirit is not confined to a physical body or limited by space; He can be present everywhere at all times.

The omniscience of the Holy Spirit is reflected in several passages, such as 1 Corinthians 2:10–11, John 14:26, and John 16:13. These verses reveal that the Holy Spirit has knowledge and understanding beyond human comprehension. He knows the depths of God's thoughts and reveals them to believers, guiding them into all truth.

The sovereignty of the Holy Spirit is evident in Zechariah 12:10, which prophecies that God will pour out His Spirit of grace and supplication on His people. This shows that the Holy Spirit has the authority and power to move and work in people's lives.

Moreover, the involvement of the Holy Spirit in creation is seen in Genesis 1:1–2, where it is stated that the Spirit of God was hovering over the waters during the process of creation. This highlights His active role in bringing forth life and order.

Furthermore, the Holy Spirit played a crucial role in enabling the writing of the Bible, as stated in 2 Peter 1:21. This verse indicates that the Holy Spirit inspired human authors to write God's Word, ensuring its reliability and authority.

Lastly, the Holy Spirit helps us recognize God's glory, according to 2 Corinthians 4:4. This verse suggests that without the work of the Holy Spirit, people would be blinded to the truth and unable to see the glorious light of Jesus Christ.

In conclusion, we can see that the Holy Spirit is known by a variety of names and titles throughout Scripture that emphasize His Divine Nature and qualities. He is called God, considered God, treated as equal to God the Father and Son, eternal, self-existent, omnipresent, omniscient, sovereign, involved with creation, involved in enabling the writing of the Bible, and instrumental in helping us recognize God's glory. Understanding these aspects of the Holy Spirit helps us appreciate His role in our lives and deepens our understanding of His significance within the Trinity.

Personal Characteristics

The Holy Spirit is frequently called a Person in the Bible to emphasize His distinctiveness. Jesus says the Holy Spirit provides life in John 6:63. John 14:26 and Romans 8:11, 16, and 26 reference the Holy Spirit as a teacher and empowerer, reinforcing the idea that the Holy Spirit is a Person.

Numerous Bible passages mention the Holy Spirit communicating with people. Acts 1:16 says the Holy Spirit communicates through David's Psalms. Peter hears the Holy Spirit directing him to Cornelius in Acts 10:19. These verses emphasize the Holy Spirit's communication and guidance. The Holy Spirit's ability to communicate with and guide individuals is a crucial aspect of His Personhood.

In John 15:26, Jesus says the Holy Spirit testifies about Him. This shows that the Holy Spirit is crucial to confirming Jesus' teachings. This testifying element of the Holy Spirit emphasizes His personality and mission. The Holy Spirit's role as a witness also serves to strengthen believers' faith and understanding of God's truth. By testifying about Jesus and guiding believers in their faith journey, the Holy Spirit plays a vital role in shaping the spiritual lives of individuals. Through His personal nature and active participation, the Holy Spirit continues to convey messages of love, truth, and guidance to humanity, drawing believers closer to God's will. It is through the Holy Spirit's presence and work that believers are empowered to live out their faith and spread the message of salvation to others.

The Holy Spirit alone understands God's thoughts, according to 1 Corinthians 2:11. The Holy Spirit's wisdom and comprehension are evident. It suggests He knows and understands beyond human understanding. The Holy Spirit's deep understanding of God's thoughts allows Him to guide believers in making decisions that align with God's will. This Divine wisdom enables believers to navigate challenges and obstacles with faith and confidence, knowing that the Holy Spirit is leading them in the right direction. Through prayer and meditation, believers can open their hearts to the Holy Spirit's guidance and experience the transformative power of His wisdom in their lives.

Isaiah 63:10 and Ephesians 4:30 reference the sorrowful Holy Spirit. This suggests He feels grief or pain when Christians disobey God. The Spirit loves Christians, according to Romans 15:30. As believers strive to align themselves with God's will and seek the guidance of the Holy Spirit, they are also called to be mindful of how their actions may affect Him. Just as the Holy Spirit can bring comfort and wisdom, He can also experience sorrow and disappointment when Christians choose to disobey God's commands. This serves as a reminder for believers to strive for obedience and to cultivate a deep relationship with the Holy Spirit through love, prayer, and meditation. By doing so, they can experience the fullness of His transformative power and guidance in their lives.

Believers are encouraged to rely on the Holy Spirit for wisdom, strength, and direction in their daily walk with God. Ultimately, by seeking obedience and cultivating a deep relationship with the Holy Spirit, Christians can experience God's transformative power in their lives.

Personal Characteristics of the Holy Spirit

1. He's referred to as a Person: John 6:63, 14:26, Romans 8:11, 16, 26, and 1 John 5:6.
2. He speaks: 2 Samuel 23:2; Acts 1:16; 8:29; 10:19; 11:12; 13:2; 21:11; 28:25–26; 1 Timothy 4:1; Hebrews 3:7–8; Revelation 2:7; 14:13; 22:17.
3. He witnesses: John 15:26.

4. He searches: 1 Corinthians 2:11.
5. He can be grieved: Isaiah 63:10; Ephesians 4:30.
6. He loves: Romans 15:30.
7. He has a mind: Romans 8:27.
8. He has intelligence: 1 Corinthians 2:10–11.
9. He can be tested: Acts 5:9.
10. He can be resisted: Acts 7:5.
11. He has a will: 1 Corinthians 2:11; 12:7–11.

Eternal Existence

The Holy Spirit's Eternal Nature is revealed in Hebrews 9:14, which states that Jesus Christ offered Himself to God through the Eternal Spirit. This verse aligns with the belief that only God can claim eternity, highlighting the Divinity of the Holy Spirit. The word "eternal" means "to a period of time without beginning or end, eternal of God."[47]

The Holy Spirit's Eternal Nature is significant because it emphasizes God's eternality. In Christianity, God is viewed as the One who has existed from eternity past to eternity future. This means He has no beginning or end and is not bound by time. Associating the Holy Spirit with this Eternal Nature reinforces the belief that the Holy Spirit is indeed Divine and part of the Godhead.

The verse mentioned in the original text implies that Jesus was offered to God through the Eternal Spirit. This suggests the existence of at least two beings (God the Father and the Holy Spirit) who possess eternal attributes. The reference to the Eternal Spirit indicates the presence of a Divine Entity that transcends time and is everlasting. This concept highlights the profound nature of Jesus' offering and underscores the eternal nature of the Spirit. It further emphasizes the Divine and timeless nature of the Triune God.

Holiness

The Holy Spirit is a central figure in both the Old Testament and the New Testament of the Bible. Inherent in His name, "Holy Spirit," is the idea of purity, holiness, and Divine power. In the Old Testament, the Holy Spirit is often referred to as the Spirit of God. He is depicted as being present at the creation of the world and as an active force in the lives of individuals and the nation of Israel. The Holy Spirit guides, empowers, and inspires God's chosen people, equipping them for their unique roles and tasks. Prophets, priests, and kings were anointed with the Holy Spirit to fulfill their God-given duties.

In the Old Testament, the Holy Spirit is portrayed as being sent by God the Father to accomplish specific purposes. For example, the Spirit comes upon individuals to give them wisdom, knowledge, and understanding. In Exodus 31:3, we read that Bezalel was filled with the Spirit of God in order to have skill, ability, and knowledge in all kinds of crafts. In Judges 6:34, we see that the Spirit of the Lord came upon Gideon, empowering him to lead Israel against their enemies. The Holy Spirit also plays a role in convicting people of sin, as seen in passages such as Psalm 51:11 where David pleads with God not to take His Holy Spirit from him after his sin with Bathsheba.

In the New Testament, the Holy Spirit takes on an even more prominent role. Jesus promised to send the Holy Spirit to His disciples after His ascension to heaven. In Acts 1:8, Jesus tells His followers that they will receive power when the Holy Spirit comes upon them and that they will be His witnesses in Jerusalem, Judea, Samaria, and to the ends of the Earth. This promise is fulfilled on the day of Pentecost, when the Holy Spirit descends upon the disciples in the form of tongues of fire.

In the New Testament, the Holy Spirit is also referred to as the Comforter or Advocate. He is depicted as a helper who comes alongside believers to guide them, teach them, and empower them for ministry. The Holy Spirit is described as being involved in various aspects of a believer's life, including sanctification, spiritual gifts, and prayer. He helps believers grow in their faith, producing spiritual fruit such as love, joy, peace, patience, kindness, goodness, faithfulness, gentleness, and self-control.

The Holy Spirit is integral to the Old Testament and New Testament narratives. In both contexts, He is portrayed as a Divine presence who empowers individuals for specific tasks and purposes. The name "Holy Spirit" itself conveys the idea of purity and holiness. Through the Holy Spirit, believers can experience a deep relationship with God and walk in His ways. Whether in the Old Testament or the New Testament, the Holy Spirit remains an essential figure who brings about transformation and enables believers to live out their faith in a powerful and impactful way.

Omnipotent (All powerful)

In Romans 15:19, the apostle Paul writes, "Through mighty signs and wonders, by the power of the Spirit of God; so that from Jerusalem, and round about unto Illyricum, I have fully preached the gospel of Christ." This verse highlights the Holy Spirit's ability to perform miracles and demonstrate His unlimited power. Various other verses throughout the Bible support this idea of the Holy Spirit's omnipotence.

One such verse is found in Luke 1:35, where the angel Gabriel tells Mary, "And the angel answered and said unto her, The Holy Ghost shall come upon thee, and the power of the Highest shall overshadow thee: therefore also that holy thing which shall be born of thee shall be called the Son of God." This passage emphasizes that it is through the power of the Holy Spirit that Mary conceives Jesus, the Son of God. This miraculous event clearly demonstrates the Holy Spirit's omnipotence, as only an all-powerful Being could bring about such a miraculous birth.

In Acts 1:8, Jesus also tells His disciples, "But ye shall receive power, after that the Holy Ghost is come upon you: and ye shall be witnesses unto me both in Jerusalem, and in all Judaea, and in Samaria, and unto the uttermost part of the earth." This verse highlights the Holy Spirit's role in empowering believers to spread the message of Jesus Christ. The Holy Spirit's power enables believers to boldly proclaim the Gospel and perform acts of service and ministry. The omnipotent nature of the Holy Spirit provides this power with no human limitations.

Furthermore, in 1 Corinthians 2:10-11, Paul writes, "But God hath revealed them unto us by His Spirit: for the Spirit searcheth all things, yea, the deep things of God. For what man knoweth the things of a man, save the spirit of man which is in him? even so the things of God knoweth no man, but the Spirit of God." This passage indicates that the Holy Spirit possesses knowledge and understanding of all things. This knowledge is not limited or restricted in any way, further emphasizing the Holy Spirit's omnipotence.

The concept of the Holy Spirit's omnipotence is not limited to these specific verses but can be found throughout the Bible. The Holy Spirit is depicted as having authority over creation, being able to perform miracles, and possessing infinite knowledge. These attributes point to an all-powerful Being Who is not bound by human limitations.

Omniscience (All knowing)

The Holy Spirit is often referred to as the omniscient or all-knowing Spirit. This concept is derived from passages such as 1 Corinthians 2:11, which states, "For what man knoweth the things of a man, save the spirit of man which is in him? even so the things of God knoweth no man, but the Spirit of God." This verse highlights the unique role of the Holy Spirit in understanding the depths of God's thoughts and intentions. It emphasizes that just as our own spirit knows our innermost thoughts, so does the Spirit of God possess complete knowledge of God's mind.

Throughout the Bible, there are numerous instances where the Holy Spirit is depicted as having omniscient attributes. For example, in John 16:13, Jesus says, "Howbeit when he, the Spirit of truth, is come, he will guide you into all truth: for he shall not speak of himself; but whatsoever he shall hear, that shall he speak: and he will shew you things to come." This verse portrays the Holy Spirit as a source of Divine wisdom and revelation. It suggests that the Spirit possesses an intimate understanding of God's plans and purposes, providing guidance and insight to believers.

In addition to this role in revealing truth and guiding believers, the Holy Spirit's omniscience is also evident in the ability to convict individuals of sin. In John 16:8, Jesus states, "And when he is come, he will reprove the world of sin, and of righteousness, and of judgment:" This verse implies that the Holy Spirit is fully aware of every sin people commit. He can convict individuals of their wrongdoing and lead them toward repentance and righteousness.

Furthermore, the Holy Spirit's omniscience is demonstrated in His role as a teacher. 1 Corinthians 2:13 says, "Which things also we speak, not in the words which man's wisdom teacheth, but which the Holy Ghost teacheth; comparing spiritual things with spiritual." This verse indicates that the Holy Spirit has the ability to teach spiritual truths and concepts to believers. It possesses comprehensive knowledge and understanding of spiritual realities, enabling it to effectively communicate these truths to those who seek wisdom and understanding.

Numerous biblical passages that emphasize the Holy Spirit's role in knowing God's thoughts, leading believers into truth, convicting people of sin, and imparting spiritual truths, support the idea that He is omniscient. The Holy Spirit's omniscience is a significant aspect of His Divine Nature and underscores His vital role in the lives of believers. Understanding and acknowledging this attribute can deepen one's relationship with the Holy Spirit and foster a greater appreciation for His wisdom and guidance.

Omnipresence (All present)

The concept of omnipresence, or being all present, is a fundamental aspect of the Holy Spirit, as depicted in Psalm 139:7 and other verses in the Bible. This Divine attribute highlights the pervasive nature of the Holy Spirit, who is present everywhere at all times. In Psalm 139:7, the psalmist acknowledges this omnipresence by saying, "Whither shall I go from thy spirit? or whither shall I flee from thy presence?" This verse emphasizes the inability to escape the presence of the Holy Spirit, indicating that no matter where one may find themselves, the Spirit is always there.

Throughout the Bible, several other verses further emphasize the omnipresence of the Holy Spirit. In 1 Corinthians 6:19, for example, it is stated that our bodies are temples of the Holy Spirit, Who dwells within us. This suggests that the Spirit is present everywhere in the world and resides within each believer. This intimate indwelling demonstrates the personal and constant presence of the Holy Spirit in every aspect of our lives.

Physical boundaries or geographical locations do not limit the Holy Spirit's presence but rather the Holy Spirit transcends all barriers to be with us at all times. This constant companionship provides us comfort, guidance, and reassurance in our daily lives, reminding us that we are never alone. As believers, we can take solace in the fact that the Holy Spirit is always with us, guiding us on our journey of faith and helping us to navigate life's challenges with wisdom and grace. The indwelling of the Holy Spirit serves as a reminder of God's unfailing love and presence in our lives, offering us strength and support in times of need.

Holy Spirit God

The Divinity and role of the Holy Spirit are acknowledged in multiple facets. In Acts 5:3-4, He is explicitly called God, solidifying His Divine nature. Furthermore, He is referred to as the Spirit of God in Genesis 1:2 and Judges 3:10, emphasizing His connection to the Almighty. The verses in Acts 28:25–27, 2 Corinthians 6:16, and Hebrews 3:7–9 further underscore His Deity, establishing Him as God. The Scriptures consistently place the Holy Spirit on equal footing with God the Father and the Son, highlighting their co-equality within the Trinity. This can be seen, as well, in passages such as Matthew 3:16, Matthew 28:19, 1 Corinthians 12:4–6, 2 Corinthians 13:14, Ephesians 2:18, Ephesians 4:4–6, and 1 Peter 1:2.

The Eternal Nature of the Holy Spirit is proclaimed in Hebrews 9:14, affirming His timeless existence. Additionally, Romans 8:2 highlights His self-existence, further solidifying His Divine attributes. The Holy Spirit's omnipresence and omniscience are revealed through Psalms 139:7–8, stating that there is no place where He is not present. Other passages, such as 1 Corinthians 2:10–11, John 14:26, and John 16:13, showcase His all-knowing characteristics. These verses emphasize the Holy Spirit's ability to be present everywhere and to possess infinite knowledge.

Zechariah 12:10 highlights the Holy Spirit's sovereignty, illustrating His authority and power. Furthermore, His involvement in creation is affirmed in Genesis 1:1–2, where it is stated that the Spirit of God was present during the creation of the world. The Holy Spirit's role in the inspiration of Scripture is acknowledged in 2 Peter 1:21, emphasizing His active role in revealing God's word to humanity. Additionally, 2 Corinthians 4:4 mentions His work in revealing the glory of God to believers, showcasing His role in illuminating spiritual truths.

Finally, 1 Corinthians 12:13 captures the Holy Spirit's active participation in the Christian life and faith. This verse highlights His ability to enable believers to confess Jesus as Lord, emphasizing His transformative power and guidance. Through His presence and influence, the Holy Spirit empowers believers to live out their faith and grow in their relationship with God.

In conclusion, the Holy Spirit's Divinity and role within the Christian faith are multifaceted and firmly established in Scripture. From His Deity and co-equality within the Trinity to His eternal Nature, omnipresence, omniscience, sovereignty, involvement in creation, inspiration of Scripture, and active participation in the Christian life, the Holy Spirit plays a vital role in the beliefs and experiences of believers.

"Holy Spirit is God" Verses:

1. The Holy Spirit is referred to as God: Acts chapter 5:3,4.
2. He is also known as the Spirit of God: Genesis 1:2; Judges 3:10.
3. He is considered God: Acts 28:25-27, 2 Corinthians 6:16, and Hebrews 3:7-9.
4. The Holy Spirit is treated as equal to God the Father and the Son: Matthew 3:16, Matthew 28:19, 1 Corinthians 12:4-6, 2 Corinthians 13:14, Ephesians 2:18, Ephesians 4:4-6, and 1 Peter 1:2.
5. He is eternal: Hebrews 9:14.
6. He is self-existent: Romans 8:2.
7. His omnipresence: Psalms 139:7-8.
8. His omniscience: 1 Corinthians 2:10-11, John 14:26, and John 16:13.
9. The Holy Spirit's sovereignty: Zechariah 12:10.
10. He was involved with creation: Genesis 1:1-2.
11. He enabled the writing of the Bible: 2 Peter 1:21.

12. He assists us in recognizing the Glory of God: 2 Corinthians 4:4.
13. He empowers believers to call upon Jesus as Lord: 1 Corinthians 12:13.

Isaiah 48:16

"Come near to me; listen to this: From the beginning I have not spoken in secret, From the time it took place, I was there. And now the LORD GOD has sent Me, and His Spirit." (NASB)

When God refers to "His Spirit," He uses the personal pronoun "His" to indicate possession. This pronoun signifies that the Spirit belongs to God. Stating that the Spirit is God's possession suggests that the Spirit is an integral part of Himself. Therefore, when God says "His Spirit," it implies that the Holy Spirit is not separate from God but an essential aspect of His Divine Nature. In later passages, we see how the Spirit empowers individuals such as Moses, David, and other prophets to carry out God's will and deliver His messages to His people. The Spirit's presence and influence in these accounts reinforce the idea that He is an inseparable part of God Himself.

The Bible teaches us that God is without sin, flaw, or imperfection. Psalm 18:30 states, "As for God, his way is perfect: the word of the LORD is tried: he is a buckler to all those that trust in him." This verse emphasizes that God's ways are faultless and His word is without error.

Similarly, Deuteronomy 32:4 says, "He is the Rock, his work is perfect: for all his ways are judgment: a God of truth and without iniquity, just and right is he." These verses highlight God's perfection.

On the other hand, angels, humans, and all other created beings are not perfect. Romans 3:23 states, "For all have sinned, and come short of the glory of God;." This verse reminds us that every human being has fallen short of God's perfection and holiness due to our sinful nature. Furthermore, Job 4:18 says, "Behold, he put no trust in his servants; and his angels he charged with folly:" This verse suggests that even angels can err and are not infallible.

Therefore, the Bible tells us that the Holy Spirit is to bring believers to the truth. There is only one perfect and Holy being, and that is God. Thus, if the Holy Spirit is not God or perfect, He can make errors and potentially lead a believer away from God. Also, blasphemy of the Holy Spirit is never a good idea!

Isaiah and Psalms

In Isaiah chapter 63, verse 10, we find a mention of the Israelites in the wilderness. This verse highlights their rebellious nature and how they grieved the Holy Spirit. It is interesting to note that in parallel verses found in Psalms 78, specifically verses 40-41, we see a similar account of the Israelites rebelling against God, grieving Him, testing His patience, and provoking the Holy One of Israel.

The question arises: who exactly did the Israelites rebel and grieve? Is there an error in the Bible? The answer is *no.* Isaiah and Psalms refer to the same Entity, albeit using different terms. In Isaiah, the reference is made to the Holy Spirit, while in Psalms, God, the Holy One of Israel, is mentioned. This emphasizes the Divine Nature of the Holy Spirit, God Himself. Thus, there is no contradiction but rather a deeper understanding of the unity and Divinity of the Holy Spirit.

It is vital to note that although Isaiah mentions the Holy Spirit while Psalms refer to God and the Holy One of Israel, the Bible is not contradictory or trying to trick someone into calling the Holy Spirit God. The Holy Spirit is an integral part of God's Triune Nature, which consists of God the Father, God the Son (Jesus Christ), and God the Holy Spirit. Therefore, when Isaiah speaks of the Israelites grieving the Holy Spirit, it is synonymous with grieving God Himself.

The Rock

In 2 Samuel 23, the phrase "The Spirit of the LORD" is identified as the "Rock" of Israel and as "The God of Israel." This chapter contains the last words of David, the great king of Israel, and provides insight into his relationship with God and his understanding of Divine guidance. Throughout his life, David experienced the presence and power of God in various ways, and in this passage, he acknowledges the role of the Spirit of the LORD in his life and leadership.

David refers to the Spirit of the LORD as the "Rock" of Israel. This metaphor highlights the strength, stability, and reliability that God provides to His people. Just as a rock serves as a firm foundation, the Spirit of the LORD empowers and supports David in his role as king. Through the guidance of the Spirit, David can lead his people with wisdom and righteousness. By identifying the Spirit as the Rock of Israel, David acknowledges that it is through God's presence and guidance that he has been able to accomplish great things.

Furthermore, David recognizes the Spirit of the LORD as "The God of Israel." This title emphasizes the Divine Nature and authority of the Spirit. It signifies that the Spirit is not merely a force or an influence, but a personal being who is worthy of worship and obedience. David understands that through his relationship with this God, he has achieved success and established his kingdom. The Spirit of the LORD is not just a source of power for David but also a source of comfort, guidance, and protection.

David considers his own life and experiences throughout 2 Samuel 23, acknowledging that the LORD's Spirit's power and presence made all of his accomplishments possible. He acknowledges that it was through Divine intervention and guidance that he was able to defeat his enemies, establish a kingdom, and lead his people.

David's humility in crediting God for his successes reminds him that true leadership requires dependence on a higher power.

Sovereign LORD

Isaiah 40:13 is a powerful verse that highlights the Nature and authority of the Spirit of the LORD. This verse states, "Who hath directed the Spirit of the LORD, or bring his counselor hath taught him?" The Spirit of the LORD mentioned here is none other than the Holy Spirit, who is an integral part of the Triune Nature of God. In Romans 11:34, the Holy Spirit is identified as the LORD when it says, "For who hath known the mind of the LORD? or who hath been his counselor?"

The identification of the Holy Spirit as the LORD in Romans 11:34 emphasizes the Deity and sovereignty of the Spirit. It implies that the Holy Spirit possesses all the attributes and authority that belong to God. The Holy Spirit is not a mere force or power but a personal being who shares in the Divine Nature. This understanding is crucial because it helps us comprehend the depth and significance of the work of the Holy Spirit in our lives and in the world.

Furthermore, Isaiah 40:13 reveals that the Spirit of the LORD is sovereign and does not answer to anyone. This verse implies that no one can fully understand God's Spirit or instruct Him on what to do. The Holy Spirit operates independently, according to His own wisdom and purpose. The verse highlights the Divine autonomy of the Holy Spirit and underscores His role as an equal member of the Triune God.

This sovereignty of the Holy Spirit has profound implications for believers. It means we cannot manipulate or control Him according to our desires or agendas. Instead, we are called to submit to His lead and guidance, recognizing that He knows what is best for us. The Holy Spirit perfectly harmonizes with God's will, bringing about His plans and purposes in our lives and within the world.

The fact that the Holy Spirit does not answer to anyone also signifies His infinite wisdom and knowledge. As Isaiah 40:13 states,

"Who hath directed the Spirit of the LORD, or being his counsellor hath taught him?" This rhetorical question emphasizes that human understanding is limited when it comes to comprehending God's Spirit. *The Holy Spirit's wisdom surpasses human understanding and enables Him to guide and empower believers in ways that are beyond our comprehension.*

Chapter 7: Trinity Clears It Up

Diving into the New Testament verses that quote the Old Testament is a truly captivating and enriching experience in Bible study. It's akin to embarking on a treasure hunt, seeking out hidden gems of wisdom and revelation. What adds an extra layer of fascination is when the Old Testament verses employ the Tetragrammaton, the sacred name of God represented by the LORD, Yahweh, or YHVH. When these verses are quoted in the New Testament and directly applied to Jesus Christ or the Holy Spirit, it opens up a whole new realm of significance and meaning.

Uncovering these connections between the Old and New Testaments is like deciphering a secret code. It unveils the deep unity and consistency of God's Word throughout the ages, demonstrating that Jesus Christ is not merely a figure of the New Testament, but rather the embodiment of God's promises and prophecies from the very beginning. It highlights the Divine inspiration behind both the Old and New Testaments, weaving together the intricate tapestry of God's plan for humanity.

Encountering New Testament verses that quote Old Testament passages using the Tetragrammaton serves as a powerful reminder of God's Eternal Nature. The Tetragrammaton embodies God's personal and covenantal name, and when applied to Jesus Christ or the Holy Spirit, it signifies their Divine identity and authority. This reveals that Jesus is not just a human teacher or prophet, but rather God in human form, dwelling among us.

Moreover, these connections between the Old and New Testaments deepen our comprehension of Jesus' role as the Messiah. They unveil how He flawlessly fulfilled the prophecies and promises of the Old Testament. It becomes evident that every aspect of Jesus' life, death, and resurrection was foretold and prefigured in the ancient scriptures. This realization fills us with awe and wonder at the intricacy of God's plan and His faithfulness to His people throughout history.

Studying these New Testament verses that quote the Old Testament also fosters a deep appreciation for the Holy Spirit's role in interpreting and applying Scripture. It serves as a reminder that the Holy Spirit inspired both the writers of the Old Testament and the writers of the New Testament. The Spirit's guidance ensures that these quotes are not mere coincidences or human interpretations, but rather Divine connections that reveal profound truths about God's Nature and His redemptive plan for humanity.

Exploring the New Testament verses that quote the Old Testament is an incredibly fulfilling Bible study pursuit. It unveils hidden treasures of wisdom, reveals the unity of God's Word, and deepens our understanding of Jesus Christ as the fulfillment of God's promises. The application of the Tetragrammaton to Jesus and the Holy Spirit adds another layer of significance and demonstrates their Divine Trinity identity. This study invites us to marvel at God's Eternal Nature, His faithfulness to His people, and His intricate plan for salvation throughout history. When faced with these profound connections, one will inevitably be led to two different conclusions.

One may find themselves pondering whether God deliberately changed the Tetragrammaton to lead people into violating the first commandment by calling Jesus and the Holy Spirit Yahweh, or if God is deliberately revealing to the readers that the Triune God is real and that Jesus, God the Father, Holy Spirit, LORD, and Yahweh are all synonyms. This contemplation invites us to delve deeper into the profound mysteries of the Divine and the intricate ways in which God reveals Himself to humanity.

One Way to Be Saved

Joel 2:23 is a prophetic passage in the Old Testament that speaks of a time when everyone who calls on the name of the LORD (YHVH) will be saved. This passage is significant because it foreshadows the new covenant established through Jesus Christ. Through the new covenant, all people would be able to experience salvation, for which Jesus' blood serves as a symbol. Romans 10:13 directly applies this prophecy to Jesus Christ, affirming that He is the fulfillment of Joel's words.

The connection between Jesus and Yahweh in this context is profound. The mention of the LORD (YHVH) in Joel's prophecy and its direct application to Jesus in Romans 10:13 suggest that Jesus is the embodiment of Yahweh. In other words, Jesus is God in human form, fulfilling the promises and prophecies of the Old Testament. This connection between Jesus and Yahweh emphasizes Jesus's Divinity and highlights His role as the Savior of humanity.

Furthermore, the fact that there is only one way to be saved, and that is through Jesus Christ, further strengthens the connection between Jesus and Yahweh. In John 14:6, Jesus Himself declares, "I am the way, the truth, and the life. No one comes to the Father except through me." This statement leaves no room for doubt or alternative paths to salvation. Jesus unequivocally proclaims Himself as the exclusive means by which humanity can be saved and reconciled with God.

We get a glimpse of which name was to be called upon. In Acts 22:16, the Apostle Paul recounts the moment he was instructed to be baptized and repent of his sins. What is remarkable about this passage is that it emphasizes the significance of invoking the name of Jesus during baptism. It was not simply a ritual or a symbolic act, but a powerful declaration of faith in Jesus Christ as Lord and Savior. By calling upon the name of Jesus during baptism, Paul acknowledges the transformative power of Christ's sacrifice on the cross and His ability to cleanse and redeem us from our sins. This verse serves as a reminder that our salvation is found in Jesus alone, and by invoking His name, we acknowledge our complete dependence on him for forgiveness and new life.

Way For The LORD

The prophecy in Isaiah 40:3-5 is a significant passage in the Old Testament that foretells the coming of the LORD. It states, "The voice of him that crieth in the wilderness, Prepare ye the way of the LORD, make straight in the desert a highway for our God. Every valley shall be exalted, and every mountain and hill shall be made low: and the crooked shall be made straight, and the rough places plain: And the glory of the LORD shall be revealed, and all flesh shall see it together: for the mouth of the LORD hath spoken it." This prophecy speaks of a messenger who will prepare the way for the LORD, making the paths straight and preparing the people for His coming.

We can clearly see references in the New Testament to Jesus Christ fulfilling this prophecy. The Gospel of Matthew, in chapter 3, verse 3, quotes this prophecy in reference to John the Baptist. It says, "This is he who was spoken of through the prophet Isaiah: 'A voice of one calling in the wilderness, 'Prepare the way for the LORD, make straight paths for him.'" Here, John the Baptist is identified as the voice calling in the wilderness, preparing the way for the LORD. This clearly connects Jesus with the fulfillment of Isaiah's prophecy.

Similarly, in Mark 1:3, we see another reference to this prophecy. It says, "The voice of one crying in the wilderness, Prepare ye the way of the LORD, make his paths straight." Again, this verse identifies John as the one fulfilling Isaiah's prophecy and preparing the way for Jesus.

Luke's Gospel also includes this prophecy in Luke 3:4-6. It says, "As it is written in the book of the words of Isaiah the prophet: 'A voice of one calling in the wilderness, 'Prepare the way for the Lord, make straight paths for him. Every valley shall be filled in, and every mountain and hill shall be made low. The crooked roads shall become straight, and the rough ways smooth. And all people will see

God's salvation.'" Like Matthew and Mark, Luke connects John's role as a messenger preparing the way for Jesus with Isaiah's prophecy.

Lastly, in John 1:23, we find another reference to this prophecy. John is asked if He is Elijah or a prophet, to which He replies, "He said, I am the voice of one crying in the wilderness, Make straight the way of the Lord, as said the prophet Isaiah." Once again, John acknowledges his role as a precursor to Jesus and directly links his mission with Isaiah's prophecy.

In conclusion, Isaiah's prophecy in chapter 40 clearly speaks of a messenger who will prepare the way for the Lord. In each of these four Gospel accounts—Matthew, Mark, Luke, and John—we see this prophecy being fulfilled by John the Baptist as he prepares people for Jesus' coming. The connection between Isaiah's prophecy and Jesus is undeniable, affirming Jesus' identity as the Lord referenced in Isaiah's words. These passages provide strong evidence that Jesus is indeed the fulfillment of Old Testament prophecies and further establish His authority and Divinity.

Tempted by the Devil

We can see the devil tempting Jesus in Matthew 4:7. This passage is significant because it reveals Jesus' response to the devil's temptations and His declaration of His Divine nature. When the devil tempts Jesus to throw himself off the pinnacle of the temple, he challenges Jesus to prove that He is the Son of God. However, Jesus responds by quoting Deuteronomy 6:16, saying, "Ye shall not tempt the LORD your God, as ye tempted him in Massah"

By quoting this scripture, Jesus rejects the devil's temptation and asserts His identity as the LORD God. Deuteronomy 6:16's original context is a warning against testing God's faithfulness during the Israelites' journey in the wilderness. However, Jesus applies this scripture to Himself, declaring that He is the LORD God Who should not be tested.

This declaration by Jesus is significant because it is the only instance in the New Testament where Jesus explicitly identifies himself as the LORD God. Jesus often referred to Himself as the Son of God or the Son of Man throughout His ministry. But in this particular passage, He emphasizes His Divine nature and authority over all things, including the devil.

Jesus' response to the devil's temptation highlights His complete dependence on and obedience to God. He shows that He will not succumb to the devil's tactics or be swayed from His mission. Instead, Jesus remains steadfast in His faith and trusts in God's plan.

Furthermore, this passage also serves as a reminder for believers today. It teaches us the importance of recognizing and resisting temptation by relying on scripture and trusting God's guidance. Just as Jesus quoted scripture to counter the devil's temptations, we, too, can find strength and wisdom in God's Word when faced with trials and temptations.

In conclusion, Matthew 4:7 showcases Jesus' response to the devil's temptation and His declaration of himself as the LORD God. By quoting Deuteronomy 6:16, Jesus affirms His Divine Nature and authority over all things. This passage reminds believers to rely on scripture and trust in God's guidance when facing temptations.

LORD Adonai

Psalms 110:1 is a significant verse in the Old Testament that is crucial to understanding Jesus's role in the Gospels. The verse states, "The LORD says to my Lord: 'Sit at my right hand until I make your enemies a footstool for your feet.'" This verse is often referred to as a messianic prophecy and is frequently quoted and alluded to in the New Testament, particularly in the Gospels.

In the Gospels, this verse is frequently applied to Jesus, especially in His interactions with the religious leaders of His time. Jesus Himself refers to this verse when He asks the Pharisees, in Matthew 22:42 "Saying, What think ye of Christ? whose son is he? They say unto him, The Son of David." By doing so, Jesus challenges their understanding of the Messiah and implies that He Himself is the fulfillment of this prophecy from Psalm 110:1.

The significance of Psalm 110:1 lies in its portrayal of Jesus as both the Son of God and the promised Messiah. The mention of "The LORD says to my Lord" suggests a conversation between God the Father and God the Son. This implies a Divine relationship between the Two, with Jesus being not just a human descendant but also sharing in the Divine Nature.

Furthermore, the phrase "Sit thou at my right hand" is significant as it denotes a position of authority and honor. In ancient Near Eastern cultures, sitting at the right hand of a king indicated being second in command. Applying this verse to Jesus indicates His exalted position and authority in relation to God the Father.

Moreover, Psalm 110:1 also speaks of Jesus' ultimate victory over His enemies. The phrase "until I make thine enemies thy footstool" suggests that Jesus will subdue and overcome all opposition. This is evident in the Gospels, where Jesus confronts and defeats various opponents, including Satan, sin, and even death itself, through His resurrection.

The Gospels apply Psalm 110:1 to Jesus, highlighting His Divinity, authority, and victory over His enemies. It emphasizes His unique role as both the Son of God and the promised Messiah. This verse serves as a powerful affirmation of Jesus' identity and mission, reinforcing His claim to be the long-awaited Savior who fulfills Old Testament prophecies.

LORD Called

In the book of Isaiah, specifically in Isaiah 42:6, the LORD is identified as the Holy Spirit. This verse states, "I the LORD have called thee in righteousness, and will hold thine hand, and will keep thee, and give thee for a covenant of the people, for a light of the Gentiles;" Here, the LORD is speaking about calling someone in righteousness and making them a covenant for the people. This description aligns with the role of the Holy Spirit as a guide and source of Divine revelation.

In Acts 13:47, we see further confirmation that the LORD mentioned in Isaiah 42:6 is indeed the Holy Spirit. In this verse, Paul and Barnabas speak to the Jewish audience and proclaim the message of salvation to them. They say, "For so hath the LORD commanded us, saying, I have set thee to be a light of the Gentiles, that thou shouldest be for salvation unto the ends of the earth.'" This statement echoes the words of Isaiah 42:6, stating that the LORD will make someone a light for the Gentiles.

Moreover, in Acts 13:2-4, we find evidence that the Holy Spirit indeed gives the order. This passage describes how the church in Antioch was worshiping and fasting when the Holy Spirit spoke to them and directed them to set apart Paul and Barnabas for a specific mission. It says, "As they ministered to the Lord, and fasted, the Holy Ghost said, Separate me Barnabas and Saul for the work whereunto I have called them. And when they had fasted and prayed, and laid their hands on them, they sent them away."

This sequence of events clearly shows that the Holy Spirit is giving the order and calling Paul and Barnabas to their mission. This aligns with Isaiah 42:6, where it is stated that the LORD will call someone in righteousness and make them a covenant for the people. The fact that the Holy Spirit speaks in this order further reinforces the identification of the LORD in Isaiah 42:6 as the Holy Spirit.

Overall, these passages from Isaiah and Acts provide clear evidence that the Holy Spirit is identified as the LORD mentioned in Isaiah 42:6. The similarities in language and purpose between these verses indicate a strong connection between them. Additionally, Acts 13:2-4 confirms that the Holy Spirit indeed gives the order and directs Paul and Barnabas to their mission. This understanding further enhances our understanding of the role and identity of the Holy Spirit in Christian theology.

LORD Judges

In Isaiah 45:23, the LORD is speaking and He is then later on identified as Jesus in Romans 14:11. The passage from Isaiah states, "I have sworn by myself, the word is gone out of my mouth in righteousness, and shall not return, That unto me every knee shall bow, every tongue shall swear." In Romans 14:11, the Apostle Paul quotes this verse and applies it directly to Jesus, saying, "For it is written, As I live, saith the Lord, every knee shall bow to me, and every tongue shall confess to God." By connecting these two passages, it becomes clear that the LORD in Isaiah 45:23 is none other than Jesus Himself.

Furthermore, Romans 11:9 supports the identification of Jesus as the LORD by stating that Christ is the Lord of both the dead and the living. This verse reads, "And David saith, Let their table be made a snare, and a trap, and a stumblingblock, and a recompence unto them." The reference to David in this verse is a quotation from Psalm 69:22-23. In this psalm, David speaks of his enemies and invokes God's judgment upon them. However, in Romans 11:9, Paul applies this passage to Christ, indicating that Jesus is the one who has authority over both the living and the dead. This further reinforces the understanding that Jesus is the LORD, as mentioned in Isaiah 45:23.

Moreover, there are several other Bible verses that clearly show Jesus as the judge of mankind. In John 5:22, Jesus Himself declares, "For the Father judgeth no man, but hath committed all judgment unto the Son." This statement emphasizes Jesus' role as the ultimate judge of humanity. In Acts 10:42, Peter also proclaims that God has appointed Jesus as the judge of the living and the dead. He says, "And he commanded us to preach unto the people, and to testify that it is he which was ordained of God to be the Judge of quick and dead." This aligns with what was previously stated in Romans 11:9.

Furthermore, in Matthew 25:31-32, Jesus describes a scene in which He will come in glory, accompanied by His angels, to judge all nations. He says, "When the Son of Man comes in his glory, and all the angels with him, then he will sit on his glorious throne. Before him will be gathered all the nations..." This vivid depiction of Jesus as the judge of all nations underscores His Divine authority and power.

In conclusion, Isaiah 45:23 clearly identifies Jesus as the LORD when it is referenced in Romans 14:11. This identification is further supported by Romans 11:9 which states that Christ is the Lord of both the dead and the living. Moreover, several other Bible verses, such as John 5:22, Acts 10:42, and Matthew 25:31-32 affirm Jesus' role as the judge of mankind. These passages collectively demonstrate that Jesus possesses ultimate authority and will serve as the judge for all people.

LORD Kingdom Reign

In Zechariah 14:17 and Isaiah 24:21-23, the term "LORD" is used to refer to Jesus in Luke 1:30–33. These passages indicate that Jesus and His Kingdom, along with His reign, are being spoken of. The identification of Jesus as the LORD in these verses supports the belief that Jesus is a human being and the Divine Son of God.

In Luke 1:30–33, the angel Gabriel appears to Mary and announces that she will conceive a Child who will be called Jesus. The angel describes Jesus as the Son of the Most High and says that He will be given the throne of His ancestor David. This reference to Jesus being given the throne of David connects Him to the messianic prophecies of the Old Testament, particularly those found in Zechariah and Isaiah.

In Zechariah 14:17, the LORD is described as coming to reign as King over all the earth. This passage speaks of all nations coming to worship the LORD during the Feast of Tabernacles. In Isaiah 24:21–23, the LORD is depicted as punishing the powers of the earth and establishing His rule over them. Both of these passages describe a future time when the LORD will establish His Kingdom and reign over all nations.

When we compare these prophecies with Luke 1:30–33, it becomes clear that Jesus is being identified as the LORD who will come to establish His Kingdom and reign over all nations. This identification further emphasizes the Divinity of Jesus and His role as the Son of God. It shows that Jesus is not just a human being but also God Himself, who will bring about His Kingdom on earth.

Furthermore, the fact that Jesus is referred to as God in these passages provides additional evidence for the concept of a Triune God. In Luke 1:32, Gabriel declares that Jesus will be called the Son of the Most High, indicating His Divine Nature. This title implies that Jesus shares in the Nature and authority of God Himself.

The concept of a Triune God, consisting of Father, Son, and Holy Spirit, is a fundamental belief in Christianity. The identification of Jesus as both LORD and God reinforces this belief by highlighting His Divine Nature and authority. It affirms that Jesus is not just a prophet or a teacher but also the second Person of the Trinity.

In conclusion, Zechariah 14:17 and Isaiah 24:21-23 identify Jesus as the LORD who will come to establish His Kingdom and reign over all nations. Luke 1:30–33, which describes Jesus as the Son of the Most High who will inherit the throne of David, further supports this identification. The use of these prophecies to refer to Jesus demonstrates His Divinity and reinforces the belief in a Triune God.

Bear Witness

In John chapter 3, Jesus is having a conversation with Nicodemus, a Pharisee and a ruler of the Jews. In this dialogue, Jesus uses plural words such as "we" and "our" when referring to the testimony that He, His Father, and the Holy Spirit bear. This usage of plural language is significant because it reveals the plurality within the Triune God: the Father, the Son (Jesus), and the Holy Spirit.

When Jesus says, "We speak of what we know and testify to what we have seen," He emphasizes the unity and agreement between Himself, God the Father, and the Holy Spirit. It is a declaration that their testimony is the same. This unity of testimony highlights Jesus' Divine Nature as equal with God.

The concept of plurality within the Triune God is further reinforced in 1 John 5:7-8, which states, "For there are three that bear record in heaven, the Father, the Word, and the Holy Ghost: and these three are one. And there are three that bear witness in earth, the Spirit, and the water, and the blood: and these three agree in one." Here, the Father, the Word (referring to Jesus), and the Holy Spirit are identified as three distinct Persons who bear witness. Yet, despite their individuality, They are also united as One.

The use of plural language by Jesus in John chapter 3 and the reference to the three witnesses in 1 John 5:7-8 serves to emphasize both the unity and diversity within the Triune God. It reveals a profound truth about the Nature of God: *that He exists in a perfect community of love and fellowship. The Father, Son, and Holy Spirit work together in perfect harmony to accomplish their Divine purposes.*

Boast in the LORD

In Jeremiah 9:23–24, the LORD is depicted as one who exercises mercy, justice, and righteousness. This passage emphasizes the character and attributes of God, highlighting His compassion, fairness, and moral uprightness. However, in 1 Corinthians 1:30–31 and 2 Corinthians 10:17, we see a connection between the LORD of Jeremiah and Jesus. In these verses, believers are encouraged to boast "in Christ." This identifies Jesus as the embodiment of the LORD's qualities of mercy, justice, and righteousness, and reveals the Divine Nature of Jesus as the Son of God.

In 1 Corinthians 1:30–31, the Apostle Paul writes, "But of him are ye in Christ Jesus, who of God is made unto us wisdom, and righteousness, and sanctification, and redemption: That, according as it is written, He that glorieth, let him glory in the Lord." Here, Paul associates Jesus with the LORD mentioned in Jeremiah. He declares that it is through Christ that believers have access to wisdom, righteousness, sanctification, and redemption. By boasting "in the Lord," believers acknowledge their reliance on Jesus and recognize Him as the source of their spiritual growth and salvation.

Similarly, in 2 Corinthians 10:17, Paul further emphasizes the connection between Jesus and the Lord. He states, "But he that glorieth, let him glory in the Lord." This sentiment echoes Jeremiah 9:23–24 and reinforces the idea that believers should find their confidence and pride in Christ. By placing their trust in Him and acknowledging His work in their lives, believers align themselves with the LORD's mercy, justice, and His righteousness.

The identification of Jesus as the embodiment of these qualities is significant because it reveals His Divine Nature. It showcases His role as the mediator between God and humanity, bringing mercy, justice, and righteousness to those who believe in Him. Through His death and resurrection, Jesus offers forgiveness for sins and a way for humanity to be reconciled with God. By boasting "in Christ," believers acknowledge the transformative power of His grace and salvation.

Furthermore, this identification of Jesus as the fulfillment of Jeremiah's depiction of the LORD highlights the continuity between the Old and New Testaments. It demonstrates that Jesus is not a separate Entity from God but an integral part of God's plan for redemption. *The qualities attributed to the LORD in Jeremiah find their ultimate expression in Jesus Christ.*

Glory of the LORD

In Isaiah 60:1, the phrase "Glory of the LORD" refers to Jesus in Ephesians 5:14. This connection between the two verses highlights the Divinity and the Messianic Nature of Jesus Christ. Isaiah 60:1 states, "Arise, shine; for thy light is come, and the glory of the LORD is risen upon thee." This verse speaks of a glorious light that comes upon the people, indicating a manifestation of God's presence and power. In Ephesians 5:14, the Apostle Paul quotes this verse, applying it directly to Jesus. He says, "Wherefore he saith, Awake thou that sleepest, and arise from the dead, and Christ shall give thee light." Here, Paul identifies Jesus as the One who brings forth the light and glory of the LORD.

The connection between Isaiah 60:1 and Ephesians 5:14 is significant because it establishes Jesus as the fulfillment of Old Testament prophecies. Throughout the Old Testament, there are numerous prophecies about a coming Messiah who would bring salvation and restoration to God's people. By linking Isaiah 60:1 to Jesus in Ephesians 5:14, Paul affirms that Jesus is the promised Messiah. He is the one who brings the light of God's glory to shine upon His people.

Furthermore, by associating Jesus with the "Glory of the LORD," Paul emphasizes His Divine Nature. The glory of God is a recurring theme in Scripture, representing His radiant presence and majesty. In Isaiah 42:8, God declares, "I am the LORD: that is my name: and my glory will I not give to another, neither my praise to graven images." By applying Isaiah 60:1 to Jesus, Paul ascribes Divine glory to Him. This reinforces the belief that Jesus is not just a human being but God Himself in human form.

Linking Jesus with the "Glory of the LORD" also highlights His role as the source of spiritual enlightenment and transformation. In Ephesians 5:14, Paul urges his readers to "awake" and "arise from the dead." This language conveys a call to spiritual awakening and renewal. By connecting this call to Isaiah 60:1 and attributing it to Jesus, Paul suggests that through Christ, people can experience true spiritual awakening and receive the light of Divine revelation.

Lastly, the phrase "Glory of the LORD" in Isaiah 60:1 refers to Jesus in Ephesians 5:14. This connection underscores Jesus' fulfillment of Old Testament prophecies, affirms His Divine Nature, and highlights His role as the source of spiritual enlightenment. Understanding this link between the two verses gives us a deeper appreciation for the significance of Jesus' identity and mission. He is the promised Messiah and God Himself, who brings forth the light and glory of the LORD upon His people.

Every Knee Will Bow

In Isaiah chapter 45, the LORD is portrayed as the One before Whom every knee will bow and every tongue will swear allegiance. This powerful declaration emphasizes the universal authority and sovereignty of the LORD. However, it is in Philippians 2:10-11 that we find a clear identification of the LORD mentioned in Isaiah as Jesus Christ.

In Philippians 2:10-11, the apostle Paul writes, "That at the name of Jesus every knee should bow, of things in heaven, and things in earth, and things under the earth; And that every tongue should confess that Jesus Christ is Lord, to the glory of God the Father." This passage directly quotes the language used in Isaiah 45, indicating a connection between the LORD mentioned in Isaiah and Jesus Christ.

The identification of Jesus as the LORD mentioned in Isaiah not only reinforces His Divinity but also underscores His role as the ultimate judge. In Isaiah 45:23, it is stated that "I have sworn by myself, the word is gone out of my mouth in righteousness, and shall not return, That unto me every knee shall bow, every tongue shall swear." In Philippians 2:10-11, this declaration is applied specifically to Jesus, indicating that He holds the authority to judge all creation.

This also highlights the continuity between the Old Testament prophecies and their fulfillment in Jesus Christ. The Apostle Paul frequently appeals to Old Testament scriptures to support his teachings about Jesus. Here, by connecting Isaiah 45 with Philippians 2:10-11, Paul demonstrates how Jesus fulfills the expectations set forth by the prophets. He is the long-awaited Messiah who has come to establish His Kingdom and bring salvation to all who believe in Him.

In conclusion, while Isaiah chapter 45 portrays the LORD before Whom every knee will bow and every tongue will swear allegiance, it is in Philippians 2:10-11 that we find a clear identification of this LORD as Jesus Christ. By making this connection, Paul affirms Jesus' Divinity, exalted position, and role as judge. This identification also underscores the continuity between Old Testament prophecies and their fulfillment in Jesus. Through Him, all creation will ultimately submit to and worship God.

LORD the Vindicator

In Hebrews 10:26-39, the author Paul draws a connection to Deuteronomy 32:36. This connection is significant as it helps us understand the role of Jesus in judgment. In Deuteronomy 32:36, it is written, "For the LORD shall judge his people, and repent himself for his servants, when he seeth that their power is gone, and there is none shut up, or left." This verse speaks of God's compassion and righteousness in judging His people.

In Hebrews, Paul uses this Old Testament passage to highlight Jesus' role as the ultimate judge. He emphasizes that Jesus is the one Who will bring justice to those who have rejected God's salvation. The verses in Hebrews 10:30-31 state, "For we know him that hath said, Vengeance belongeth unto me, I will recompense, saith the Lord. And again, The Lord shall judge his people. It is a fearful thing to fall into the hands of the living God." Paul is making it clear that Jesus, as the living God, will execute judgment on those who have turned away from Him.

The connection between Hebrews 10:26-39 and Deuteronomy 32:36 becomes even more apparent when we consider that the Bible tells us God the Father does not judge anyone. In John 5:22, Jesus himself declares, "For the Father judgeth no man, but hath committed all judgment unto the Son." This verse affirms that judgment is delegated to Jesus. Therefore, when Paul connects these passages, he highlights Jesus' authority as the judge.

By referencing Deuteronomy 32:36 and emphasizing Jesus' role as the judge, Paul is conveying a strong message to his readers. He wants them to understand that rejecting Jesus and turning away from His salvation is a serious matter.

First and Last

Isaiah 41:4 is a powerful verse highlighting God's plurality in Nature. In this verse, God declares, "Who hath wrought and done it, calling the generations from the beginning? I the LORD, the first, and with the last; I am he." This statement reveals a deep understanding of the Divine Nature and the relationship between the Triune God. We see that the LORD here declares He is the first and that He is "with" the last. Notice the use of the first-person personal pronoun "He" in this verse. For example, this can be understood as the Father declaring His eternal existence as the first, "with" the Son as the last, and the Holy Spirit as "He" who is with them both. This verse beautifully illustrates the concept of the Trinity: the first is "with" the last, and the first and the last are "He."

The use of the terms "First" and "Last" in this verse is significant. Throughout the Old Testament, these titles are often used to refer to God the Father. They denote His eternal Nature, His preeminence, and His sovereignty over all things. However, we find a similar proclamation from Jesus Christ Himself in the book of Revelation. In Revelation 1:8, Jesus states, "I am the Alpha and the Omega, the Beginning and the End, says the Lord, who is and who was and who is to come, the Almighty." Here, Jesus takes on the titles that were previously attributed to God the Father in the Old Testament.

Isaiah 41:4 is a profound verse that reveals the plurality within God's Nature. The first refers to God the Father, while "with the last" most likely points to Jesus Christ. Though distinct, they are unified as one "He." This verse emphasizes both their unity and their distinct roles within the Trinity.

Faithful Witness

Revelation 3:14 describes Jesus as the "faithful and true witness," and Jeremiah 42:5 says, "The LORD be a true and faithful witness between us." The same title is used to identify the LORD and Jesus. This connection emphasizes Jesus' Divine Nature and authority as the LORD, the creator God.

Furthermore, Revelation 3:14 refers to Jesus as "the beginning of the creation of God," indicating that God the Father created His body through the virgin birth. This miraculous birth ensured that Jesus had a sinless body, free from the inheritance of Adam's sin, known as the original sin. The significance of this sinless body is supported by Hebrews 10:5, which mentions, "but a body hast thou prepared me" indicating that it was a specific earthly body of flesh that was created for Jesus.

Additionally, Colossians 1:15 describes Jesus as "the firstborn of every creature," reflecting His preeminence and Divine Nature. This signifies that everyone who is "born again" comes after Jesus, highlighting His role as the ultimate example and leader for those who follow Him.

These interconnected references from different parts of the Bible emphasize the Divine Nature of Jesus, His unique role in creation, and His sinless state, providing a deeper understanding of His significance in the Christian faith as fully God and fully human.

Lastly, Colossians 1:16: "For by him were all things created, that are in heaven, and that are in earth, visible and invisible, whether they be thrones, or dominions, or principalities, or powers: all things were created by him, and for him:" So if you read this verse and come to the conclusion that Jesus is not the creator God, then Satan may have a firm hold of you!

LORD My Salvation

In Exodus 15:2, the term "LORD" refers to God as "my salvation." This verse highlights the understanding that God is the source of salvation for His people. However, in Acts 4:12, this same LORD is identified as Jesus. This connection between the two passages reveals that Jesus is the embodiment of the LORD and this LORD is "my salvation." It emphasizes that there is only one way to be saved, and that is through Jesus, who is the LORD.

Salvation is consistently tied to a personal relationship with God throughout the Bible. In the Old Testament, God's people looked to Him as their source of deliverance and rescue. The term "LORD" used in Exodus 15:2 signifies God's Divine name, indicating His power and authority. This verse reminds us that salvation ultimately only comes from God alone.

However, in the New Testament, Jesus is identified as the Savior. Acts 4:12 states that "there is salvation in no one else, for there is no other name under heaven given among men by which we must be saved." Here, the Apostle Peter affirms that Jesus is the only Way to be saved. This declaration aligns with Jesus' own words in John 14:6 when He says, "Jesus saith unto him, I am the way, the truth, and the life: no man cometh unto the Father, but by me."

Charge of the Angels

In Psalms 91:9-11, it is written that the LORD has charge over His angels. This passage reflects the Divine authority and sovereignty of the LORD over the heavenly hosts. In the Gospel of Matthew 31:41, Jesus is identified as the LORD, as referenced in Psalms 91, where it is proclaimed that Jesus gives charge over His angels.

This connection between Psalms 91 and the Gospel of Matthew underscores the profound unity and identity of Jesus with the Divine LORD of the Old Testament. It serves as a powerful testament to the continuity and fulfillment of Scripture, highlighting the eternal nature of God's authority and the redemptive mission of Jesus Christ.

This exploration invites us to contemplate the deep significance of Jesus' role as the LORD who exercises Divine authority over the angelic realm, providing assurance and protection to those who trust Him. It illuminates the interconnectedness of the Old and New Testaments, revealing the timeless truth of God's sovereign care and guardianship over His people.

Chapter 8: Patristic Contributions to Trinitarian Doctrine

The term Trinity refers to a sacred doctrine that holds that the Father, the Son, and the Holy Spirit, are three yet one—not one in purpose, but one in essence. The term Trinity comes from the Latin *trinus*, meaning "threefold." The Triune Nature of God is known as the Godhead.

Bible scholars today agree that the term Trinity refers to the Father, the Son, and the Holy Spirit—but has it always been so? The Trinity doctrine has been disputed for almost 2000 years. Though early fourth-century church leaders formally affirmed that belief in the Trinity is a fundamental aspect of the Christian faith, many continue to dispute the doctrine.

Contemporaries who dispute the Trinity doctrine

- **Dennis A. Beard:** A noted author and speaker, Beard rejects the Trinity doctrine, writing, "The Doctrine of the Trinity did not exist until 325 A.D."[48]

- **Dan Brown:** Brown is a popular author who identifies as a Christian but rejects the Trinity doctrine. He argues: "Jesus' establishment as 'the Son of God' was officially proposed and voted on by the Council of Nicaea... [325 A.D. It was] a relatively close vote at that...By officially endorsing Jesus as the Son of God, Constantine turned Jesus into a Deity who existed beyond the scope of the human world, an entity whose power was unchallengeable."[49] Note: The vote was not close—the vote to affirm the Divinity of Christ carried by a 99% margin.

• **P. R. Lackey:** Known for his book, The Tyranny of the Trinity: The Orthodox Cover-Up, Lackey suggests that the Trinity doctrine was an afterthought—a late addition to the collection of accepted holy doctrine. He writes: "[At Nicaea] a whole new theology was formally canonized into the Church."[50]

• **Robert Spears:** mischaracterized the historical record when he wrote: "It is an unquestionable historical fact that the doctrine of the Trinity is a false doctrine foisted into the Church during the third and fourth centuries; which finally triumphed by the aid of persecuting emperors."[51] Spears' statement is inaccurate; the doctrine was affirmed in the fourth century but was known for centuries before that, and though some emperors persecuted believers in the early days of the New Testament Church, the emperors in question supported, endorsed, and helped to advance the cause of Christ.

• **Rob Bell:** Questioning the legitimacy of the Trinity doctrine and suggesting it was not a part of the teaching of the disciples and early church fathers, Bell argues: "This three-in-oneness understanding of God emerged in the several hundred years after Jesus' resurrection. People began to call this concept the Trinity. The word trinity is not found anywhere in the Bible. ...It was added later."[52]

It is true that the word "trinity" is not found in Scripture—but neither are the terms rapture or missions. Though the English terms do not appear in the ancient writings, most can easily see there is a solid biblical foundation for believing that God calls His people to support mission work; that God wants all believers to be spiritually prepared for the rapture; and that God has revealed His Triune Nature through what believers today call the Trinity doctrine.

The Trinity doctrine has a solid biblical foundation—*in both the Old and New Testaments.* Through progressive revelation, in His perfect timing, God provides insight into the mysteries of His Nature and faith. For example, the full significance of the Passover celebration—instituted in the days of Moses—was revealed only after the crucifixion and resurrection of Jesus. Similarly, the Trinity was revealed in Old Testament times but was not fully understood until the establishment of the New Testament Church.

This chapter will profile the history of the development of the Trinity doctrine, how it was acknowledged well before the fourth-century Council at Nicaea, and how it was affirmed throughout the centuries which followed.

The Old Testament foundation for the Trinity doctrine

The truth that God is more than One is revealed in the first verse of the Bible. Don Stewart's Blue Letter Bible notes that the word "God" in Genesis 1:1 ("In the beginning, God created the heavens and the earth") is plural. He writes:

> "The Hebrew word for God is Elohim. Elohim is a plural noun, but it is used here with a singular verb bara. In the remainder of the Old Testament, when Elohim speaks of the true God, it is always used with a singular verb. The conclusion to be drawn is that in some sense God is both singular and plural. The doctrine of the Trinity states this - within the nature of the one God there are three eternal Persons."[53]

The Multidimensional Nature of God

- "Then God said, "Let us make man in our image..." (Genesis 1:26).

- "Then I heard the voice of the Lord, saying, "Whom shall I send, and who will go for us?" (Isaiah 6:8).

- "For your Maker is...the LORD of hosts...the Holy One of Israel is your Redeemer, the God of the whole earth..." (Isaiah 54:5). Note: The word "Maker" is plural in the Hebrew text.

- Isaiah 48:16-17 references the Triune Nature of God as "The Lord God," "his Spirit," and "thy Redeemer."

Old Testament era Hebrews understood that Scripture indicates God is more than one. And they perceived the connection between the working of God and the working of the Spirit, who shared in the work of creation in Genesis along with the redemptive work of God (as a pillar of fire) in the days of Moses. However, the Hebrews of old also adopted a key verse, Deuteronomy 6:4-5, which begins, "The Lord our God is **one**."

The **one yet more** aspect of God's Nature is a mystery—it transcends human intellect and imagination. Nevertheless, Hebrews saw that Scripture points to the Multidimensional Nature of God and that the Father is intimately linked to the Holy Spirit. With the coming of the Christ, Who referred to Himself as the "I Am,"[54] and Who was referenced as Immanuel (meaning, God with us)[55] and Who fulfilled Isaiah's Messianic prophecies thus assuming the titles, "Mighty God, "Lord of lords, and King of kings;"[56] God revealed that Jesus is the third facet of the Triune Nature of God.

Jesus did not claim to be like God, or to be a spokesperson for God—He claimed to be God. Indeed, he said, "If you have seen me you have seen the Father"[57] and, "I and the Father are one."[58]

New Testament writers were moved by the Spirit to emphasize the Oneness of God and the Divinity of Christ in their writings. A few examples follow and this list is extensive, but not exhaustive. It is provided to substantiate the claim that the early church understood and believed in the Divinity of Christ.

- "In the beginning was the Word, and the Word was with God, and the Word was God." (John 1:1).

- "For this cause, therefore, the Jews were seeking all the more to kill Him, because He not only was breaking the Sabbath but also was calling God His own Father, making Himself equal with God." (John 5:18).

- "Jesus said to them, 'Truly, truly, I say to you, before Abraham was born, I am.'" (John 8:58) Note: The Jews understood this to be a claim to Deity and immediately moved to stone him for blasphemy.

- "Thomas answered and said to Him, "My Lord and my God!" (John 20:28).

- "For in Him all the fullness of Deity dwells in bodily form." (Colossians 2:9).

- "Have this attitude in yourselves which was also in Christ Jesus, who, although He existed in the form of God, did not regard equality with God a thing to be grasped, but emptied Himself, taking the form of a bond-servant..." (Philippians 1:5b-6a).

Jesus is presented as having Divine attributes. He is...

● **The Creator:** John 1:3: 1 Corinthians 8:6: Colossians 1:16-17: Hebrews 1:2; Revelation 3:14.

● **Unchanging:** Hebrews1:10-12, 13:8.

● **Eternal:** John 1:1, 8:58;17:5; Colossians 1:17; Hebrews 1:2.

● **Omniscient:** John 16:30.

● **Omnipresent**: Matthews 18:20, 28:20; John 3:13; Ephesians1:23, 4:10; Colossians 3:11.

In the second century, leaders in the Christian Church wrote and taught extensively on the Deity of Christ and His Oneness with the Father. Theophilus, bishop of Antioch, writing to Autolycus (ca. 180) was the first to employ the term *trias* ("triad") of the Godhead.[59]

Church leaders of this Era Affirming the Deity of Christ and His Oneness with God:

- **Clement of Rome** (d. c. 99). [Writing of Moses' foreshadowing of the sacrifice of Jesus]: "This was done so that the name of the true and only God [Jesus] might be glorified, to whom be the glory forever and ever. Amen."[60]

- **Aristides** (c. 125): "For they [Christians] know God, the Creator and Fashioner of all things through the only-begotten Son and the Holy Spirit; and beside Him they worship no other God."[61]

- **Theophilus of Antioch** (d. c. 185): "And I pray for favor from the only God, that I may accurately speak the whole truth according to His will, that you and everyone who reads this work may be guided by His truth and favor."[62]

- **Irenaeus of Lyons** (d. c. 202): "It is proper, then, that I should begin with the first and most important head, that is, God the Creator, who made the heaven and the earth, and all things that are therein . . . and to demonstrate that there is nothing either above Him or after Him; nor that, influenced by anyone, Lord, the only Creator, the only Father, alone containing all things, and Himself commanding all things into existence."[63]

o **Irenaeus:** "Now, that this God is the Father of our Lord Jesus Christ, Paul the apostle also has declared, [saying,] 'There is one God, the Father, who is above all, and through all things, and in us all.' I have indeed proved already that there is only one God; but I shall further demonstrate this from the apostles themselves, and from the discourses of the Lord."[64]

o **Irenaeus:** "...These [the Apostles] have all declared to us that there is one God, Creator of heaven and earth, announced by the law and the prophets; and one Christ the Son of God. If anyone does not agree to these truths, he despises the companions of the Lord; anymore, he despises Christ Himself the Lord; yea, he despises the Father also, and stands self-condemned, resisting and opposing his own salvation, as is the case with all heretics."[65]

• **Tertullian** (c. 160–225): "For God alone is without sin; and the only man without sin is Christ, since Christ is also God."[66]

o **Tertullian:** "Thus Christ is Spirit of Spirit, and God of God, as light of light is kindled... That which has come forth out of God is at once God and the Son of God...He is Spirit of Spirit and God of God... This ray of God, then, as it was always foretold in ancient times, descending into a certain virgin, and made flesh in her womb, is in His birth God and man united."[67]

o **Tertullian:** "The Father is God, and the Son is God, and the Holy Ghost is God, and each is God..."[68]

o **Tertullian:** [in response to the false teachings of Hermogenes who taught that matter was eternal and thus, not created by God and Jesus Christ]: "This rule is required by the nature of the One only God, who is One-only in no other way than as the sole God; and in no other way sole, than as having nothing else with Him. So also He will be first, because all things are after Him; and all things are after Him, because all things are by Him; and all things are by Him, because they are of nothing: so that reason coincides with the Scripture, which says: 'Who hath known the mind of the Lord? or who hath been His counselor? or with whom took He counsel? or who hath shown to Him the way of wisdom and knowledge? Who hath first given to Him, and it shall be recompensed to him again?' Surely none! Because there was present with Him no power, no material, no nature which belonged to any other than Himself."[69]

• **Ignatius of Antioch** (c. 50–117): "For our God, Jesus the Christ, was conceived by Mary according to God's plan, both from the seed of David and of the Holy Spirit."[70]

o **Ignatius:** "Consequently all magic and every kind of spell were dissolved, the ignorance so characteristic of wickedness vanished, and the ancient kingdom was abolished when God appeared in human form to bring the newness of eternal life."[71]

o **Ignatius:** "I glorify Jesus Christ, the God who made you so wise, for I observed that you are established in an unshakable faith, having been nailed, as it were, to the cross of the Lord Jesus Christ."[72]

o **Ignatius:** "Wait expectantly for Jesus, the one who is above time: the Eternal, the Invisible, who for our sake became visible; the Intangible, the Unsuffering, who for our sake suffered, who for our sake endured in every way."[73]

• **Polycarp of Smyrna** (69–155): "Now may the God and Father of our Lord Jesus Christ, and the eternal high priest himself, the Son of God Jesus Christ, build you up in faith and truth . . . and to us with you, and to all those under heaven who will yet believe in our Lord and God Jesus Christ and in His Father who raised him from the dead."[74]

• **Justin Martyr** (100–165): "And that Christ being Lord, and God the Son of God...He is called the begotten Word of God, is even God...He is God..."[75]

• **Tatian** (110–172): "We do not act as fools, O Greeks, nor utter idle tales when we announce that God was born in the form of man."[76]

• **Melito of Sardis** (d. c. 180): "He that hung up the earth in space was Himself hanged up; He that fixed the heavens was fixed with nails; He that bore up the earth was born up on a tree; the Lord of all was subjected to ignominy in a naked body – God put to death! ...The luminaries turned away, and the day darkened—because they slew God, who hung naked on the tree. . . This is He who made the heaven and the earth, and in the beginning, together with the Father, fashioned man; who was announced by means of the law and the prophets; who put on a bodily form in the Virgin; who was hanged upon the tree; who was buried in the earth; who rose from the place of the dead, and ascended to the height of heaven, and sitteth on the right hand of the Father."[77]

● **Irenaeus of Lyons** (120–202): "For I have shown from the Scriptures, that no one of the sons of Adam is as to everything, and absolutely, called God, or named Lord. But that He is Himself in His own right, beyond all men who ever lived, God, and Lord, and King Eternal, and the Incarnate Word, proclaimed by all the prophets, the apostles, and by the Spirit Himself, may be seen by all who have attained to even a small portion of the truth. Now, the Scriptures would not have testified these things of Him, if, like others, He had been a mere man...He is the holy Lord, the Wonderful, the Counselor, the Beautiful in appearance, and the Mighty God, coming on the clouds as the Judge of all men—all these things did the Scriptures prophesy of Him."[78]

o **Irenaeus:** "Christ Jesus [is] our Lord, and God, and Savior, and King, according to the will of the invisible Father."[79]

o **Irenaeus:** "Christ Himself, therefore, together with the Father, is the God of the living, who spoke to Moses, and who was also manifested to the fathers."[80]

o **Irenaeus:** "He received testimony from all that He was very man, and that He was very God, from the Father, from the Spirit, from angels, from the creation itself, from men, from apostate spirits and demons."[81]

• **Clement of Alexandria** (c. 150–215): "This Word, then, the Christ, the cause of both our being at first (for He was in God) and of our well-being, this very Word has now appeared as man, He alone being both, both God and man—the Author of all blessings to us; by whom we, being taught to live well, are sent on our way to life eternal. . . . The Word, who in the beginning bestowed on us life as Creator when He formed us, taught us to live well when He appeared as our Teacher; that as God He might afterwards conduct us to the life which never ends."[82]

• **Hippolytus** (170–235): "The Logos alone of this God is from God himself; wherefore also the Logos is God, being the substance of God."[83]

• **Origen** (c. 185–254): "Jesus Christ...in the last times, divesting Himself (of His glory), became a man, and was incarnate although God, and while made a man remained the God which He was."[84]

• **Novatian of Rome** (210–280): "For Scripture as much announces Christ as also God, as it announces God Himself as man. It has as much described Jesus Christ to be man, as moreover it has also described Christ the Lord to be God...Let them, therefore, who read that Jesus

Christ the Son of man is man, read also that this same Jesus is called also God and the Son of God."[85]

These statements were made in connection to, not independent of, the long-held understanding that the Father (God) is more than One and that He is linked to the Spirit. The New Testament writings, and the writings of early Church fathers, clarified that Jesus is also part of the multidimensional God. He is not a god, or another God; He, along with the Father and the Spirit, *is God*. The Godhead, comprised of the Father, Son, and Spirit, are three, yet one.

The Deity of Christ was a threat to the enemy, and accordingly, it was attacked on multiple fronts. A diminished understanding of the nature of Christ diminishes the need to surrender and yield to Christ. Some infiltrated the church and challenged the doctrine from within. In 318, a charismatic man named Arius in Alexandria, Egypt, publicly challenged his bishop on his views regarding the nature of Christ. His powerful oratory skills led many to follow him. The dispute grew, and a great schism began to develop. By 325, the controversy had swept across the Roman Empire, and church leaders needed to meet and resolve the matter by issuing a declarative statement on the matter. This brings us to the first great Christian Council, the Council of Nicaea.

The Council of Nicaea

The Fourth of July 1776 is a landmark day in American history—it changed the history of the world. But almost fourteen centuries earlier, on July 4, 325 A.D., about 300 Christian bishops and deacons, primarily from the eastern realm of the Roman Empire, gathered in Nicaea to discuss the important issue of the Divinity of Christ. The outcome of that meeting also had a profound impact on the world.

Nicaea was a small town near the Bosporus Straits flowing between the Black Sea and the Mediterranean. The meeting of church leaders was unprecedented—since the latter part of the first century, the Church had been sorely oppressed—millions had been jailed and martyred for their faith under ten particularly brutal Roman emperors. But in 312, Emperor Constantine reportedly converted to Christianity and lifted oppressive laws. He encouraged open worship, prayer, study, and funded the building of churches. Additionally, he led by inviting ministry leaders from across the region to come to Nicaea to bring resolution to the issue of the nature of Jesus Christ. Constantine was concerned about the growing lack of unity in the Church, warning church leaders in his introductory remarks: "Division in the church is worse than war."

Athanasius and Alexander were among the church leaders attending the Council; they called for the issue to be resolved by establishing a new creed, which would be taught to believers across the Empire. The well-respected Eusebius of Caesarea was also in attendance; he put forward his recommendation for a creed—it was the first step in formally affirming the Divinity of Christ.

Eusebius was on the right track, but some at the Council pressed for stronger language to minimize the probability of questions arising in the future. Phrases such as "True God of true God," "begotten not made," and "of one substance with the Father," were added to the draft of the creed. The Latin phrase, *homo ousion*, meaning "one substance," was also incorporated into a later draft.

After much prayer and debate, 99% of the bishops present voted to adopt a creedal statement that unequivocally affirmed the Deity of Christ (see below):

The Nicene Creed of 325

We believe in one God, the Father almighty, Maker of heaven and earth,
and of all things visible and invisible.
And in one Lord Jesus Christ, the Son of God, the only-begotten,
begotten of the Father before all ages.
Light of Light, true God of true God, begotten not made,
of one essence with the Father by whom all things were made;
who for us men and for our salvation, came down from heaven,
and was incarnate of the Holy Spirit and the Virgin Mary
and became man.
And He was crucified for us under Pontius Pilate,
and suffered, and was buried.
And the third day He rose again, according to the Scriptures;
and ascended into heaven, and sits at the right hand of the Father;
and He shall come again with glory to judge the living and the
dead;
whose Kingdom shall have no end.
And in the Holy Spirit

However, efforts to diminish the nature of Christ persisted, necessitating the coordination of future Council meetings to bring further clarity and understanding of the nature of the Godhead. A brief profile follows:

- **The First Council of Constantinople:** Emperor Theodosius I (379-395) coordinated the First Council of Constantinople in 381. The goal was to facilitate complete unity across the Empire regarding the Deity of Christ and the Trinity doctrine. At this Council, Church leaders affirmed the Trinity and developed formal statements regarding the nature and role of the Holy Spirit. The Council of Constantinople condemned all forms of Arianism (the anti-trinitarian teachings of Arius) and expanded the Nicene Creed. A listing of a few of the additions follows:

- **Regarding Jesus:** "He was incarnate by the Holy Spirit and of the Virgin Mary and was made man; he was crucified for us under Pontius Pilate, and suffered and was buried, and the third day he rose again, according to the scriptures, and ascended into heaven, and sits at the right hand of the Father."

- **Regarding baptism:** "We acknowledge one baptism for the remission of sins; we look for the resurrection of the dead, and the life of the world to come."

- **Regarding the Spirit:** "...The Holy Spirit, the Lord and giver of life...proceeds from the Father, who with the Father and the Son is worshipped and glorified, ...[and was] spoken of through the Prophets." The last paragraph of the expanded creed reads:

And [we believe] in the Holy Spirit, the Lord, the Giver of Life,
Who proceeds from the Father; who with the Father and the Son
together is worshipped and glorified; who spoke by the prophets.
In one Holy...[universal] Church.
I acknowledge one baptism for the remission of sins.
I look for the resurrection of the dead, and the life
of the world to come.

Amen.

● **Emperor Theodosius II coordinated the Council at Ephesus in 431:** At this Council, Cyril of Alexandria led church leaders to condemn the views of Nestorius, who taught that Jesus has two distinct natures, which cannot be simultaneously present.

● **Emperor Marcian and Pope Leo I coordinated the Council at Chalcedon in 451:** This Council built on the foundation laid at the Council at Ephesus by affirming that Jesus has two (simultaneous) natures—He is 100% Divine and 100% human at the same time. His nature is wonderfully mysterious and unique. The Council also condemned the anti-Trinitarian teachings of Nestorius and Eutyches.

● **Emperor Justinian coordinated the second Council at Constantinople in 553:** The Council was convened to formally condemn the view that Jesus had only one nature (monophysitism).

● **A Conference was called in the 8th century to address what was called, the Filioque Controversy:** Questions regarding the relationship between the Son and the Spirit were resolved via the term *Filioque*, Latin for "from or through the Son." Church leaders adopted the following phrase: "The Spirit is the Lord and giver of life who proceeds from the Father, and through the Son" (Latin: filioque).

Many future gatherings of key Church leaders built on the foundation laid at the first Council of Nicaea in 325. The foundational doctrines affirmed at the first Council meeting included:

- The Divinity of Christ.

- The Triune Nature of God.

- The Trinity doctrine affirms that the Father, the Son, and the Holy Spirit were three distinct aspects of God, yet all are one with and co-equal to God.

- Bishops Gregory of Nyssa, Basil of Caesarea, and Gregory Nazianzus led the Church in the fourth century to establish clear language for what has come to be known as the Trinity doctrine.

Though some of the terminology regarding the Deity of Christ and aspects of the Trinity doctrine flowed from the Council of Nicaea in 325, an understanding of the Godhead is clearly present in New Testament writings, and an understanding of the multidimensional nature of God can be traced back to Genesis 1:1.

Church leaders at the Council of Nicaea did not invent the Trinity doctrine, they affirmed, clarified, and formalized teachings that had long before been established in Scripture and affirmed by early Church leaders.

Chapter 9: Trinity and Pagan Roots

The Argument

Many argue that Christian teachings, including the foundational doctrine of the Trinity, have pagan roots. Those who hold this view argue that many stories in the Bible, as well as some Christian doctrines, find their foundation in the mythologies of other cultures. Indeed, the argument is that in some cases, key Jewish and Christian teachings are but thinly disguised plagiarisms from stories penned hundreds of years before by notables in Egyptian, Greek, Sumerian, and other cultures.

Ancient Mythologies

The Trinity doctrine: Some important Christian doctrines were formalized hundreds of years after the crucifixion of Jesus Christ. The Trinity doctrine, for example, was formalized at the Council of Nicaea in 325 A.D, and refined at subsequent Councils through the eighth century. Christians argue that the apparent late formalization of the Trinity doctrine can be attributed to the fierce oppression the early New Testament Church experienced, and does not indicate the teaching was not known and embraced immediately following Pentecost. Skeptics assert the Trinity doctrine has its foundation in Sumerian and Egyptian mythologies, which predates the Christian teaching by more than two thousand years.

The story of Jesus: Regarding the account of the ministry of Christ: hundreds of years before the Gospel writers penned their accounts, the Greeks told of a story they saw written in the constellations of heaven. Their story noted that Orion, the son of a powerful god, loved humanity in general and the Pleiades (a cluster of seven stars depicted as women) in particular. Orion embarked on a great journey to help the Pleiades, during which he showed himself to be master of the elements by walking on water and having dominion over the lake of fire.

He was confronted by, and battled, an evil beast, who injured him, bruising him on the heel. In the end, however, the son of the great god prevailed, besting the beast via a mighty blow to his head. Many argue Orion's story strongly parallels the story of Jesus, the Son of God, who journeyed to earth to show His love for humanity, walked on water, showed His authority over the elements, battled the beast (who, according to Genesis 3:15b, would "bruise His heel"), and overcame all of it via the resurrection (fulfillment of the Genesis 3:15a prophecy, which foretold the Messiah would "bruise" his "head").

The Flood story

Moses wrote the account of the Flood approximately 1450 years before the birth of Christ. However, hundreds of years before the birth of Moses, in ancient Mesopotamia, the Sumerians carved a flood story into clay tablets. Found in the late 1800s, the account has been called the Eridu Genesis. In that story, the god Enki is aware of an impending flood. He discusses the matter with other gods, who are not pleased with humanity and decide to not warn humans of the imminent danger.

Enki, however, had compassion on humanity and warned one man, Ziusudra (later known as Akkadian or Atrahasis) about the coming calamity. According to some accounts, Enki told Ziusudra to build an Ark to save humanity and the animals. The fierce storms brought torrential rains for seven days and seven nights. Some accounts have the boat coming to rest on a mountain, and other accounts have the boat floating down the Euphrates into what is now the Persian Gulf. In all accounts, the sun appears after the storm, flood waters abate, and Ziusudra exits the boat and sacrifices oxen and sheep to the gods.

It is not difficult to see the parallels between the Eridu Genesis flood story and Moses' account of Noah, written hundreds of years later.

A General Approach to Reconciling

Though some material in the Bible (and some Christian doctrines) may appear to have drawn inspiration from well-known epics from other cultures predating Old and New Testament writings, that does not prove that stories from other cultures impacted biblical writings or the development of Christian doctrines.

Notably, creation and flood stories are found in many ancient cultures. And many of these stories were written or shared via oral tradition at a time when these cultures had no contact with each other. The only explanation is that at one time, before the development of written language, there was one collection of oral stories concerning creation, the Flood, and the historical events noted in the book of Genesis. Evil corrupted the integrity of these stories after the splintering of language and culture noted in the biblical story of the Tower of Babel.[86] Moses recaptured the truth in writing Genesis.

TRINITY BELIEFS IN ANCIENT CULTURES

Honest researchers are quick to acknowledge that many ancient cultures from across the globe developed trinity-themed stories. Stories of deities taking human form, heroic figures being the son of a god, the son of a god battling evil, the son of a god being resurrected, and god revealing himself in different forms can be found in ancient Egyptian, Assyrian, Babylonian, Greek, Indian, and South African lore. A brief profile of a few notable trinity-themed stories in mythology follows:

Isis, Osiris, and Horus

According to the Heliopolitan tradition (the Greek account of Egyptian mythology), Osiris[1] became the ruler of Egypt over the objections of his elder brother Set[2]. Set seethed in anger and decided to kill Osiris after he announced he was leaving the kingdom for a time and would be leaving his wife Isis (rather than Set), in charge in his absence.

Set found an opportunity to move forward with his plan to kill his brother. One day, Set tricked Osiris into climbing into a wooden chest, then sealed the box, cut him into pieces, and threw the pieces into the Nile. Isis searched for Osiris and found the pieces of his dismembered body, which she carried back to Egypt.

Isis placed Osiris' body in the temple, and supernaturally, without a male anatomy part, became pregnant and conceived Heru-sa-aset[3] (Horus), whose destiny was to defeat Set[4].

Isis then implored the god Thoth[5] to resurrect Osiris[6]. Thoth and Isis conducted a "Ritual of Life" and set a plan in place to resurrect Osiris. However, Set discovered their plan and stole the pieces of Osiris' body and scattered them across the land of Egypt.

Isis and her sister Nephthys[7] were able to retrieve all but one of the pieces of Osiris, and with the help of Anubis[8] and Ra[9], resurrected Osiris[10], who became King of the Underworld.

---

1. https://ancientegyptonline.co.uk/osiris/

2. https://ancientegyptonline.co.uk/set/

3.   https://ancientegyptonline.co.uk/horuschild/

4.   https://ancientegyptonline.co.uk/set/

5.   https://ancientegyptonline.co.uk/thoth/

6.   https://ancientegyptonline.co.uk/osiris/

7.   https://ancientegyptonline.co.uk/nephthys/

8.   https://ancientegyptonline.co.uk/anubis/

9.   https://ancientegyptonline.co.uk/ra/

Isis gave birth to Horus and hid him in the marshes of the delta—and raised him in secret. When Horus[11] came of age, he set out to avenge the death of his father. Horus bested Set in battle and was henceforth banished to the sky by Osirus and Ra.

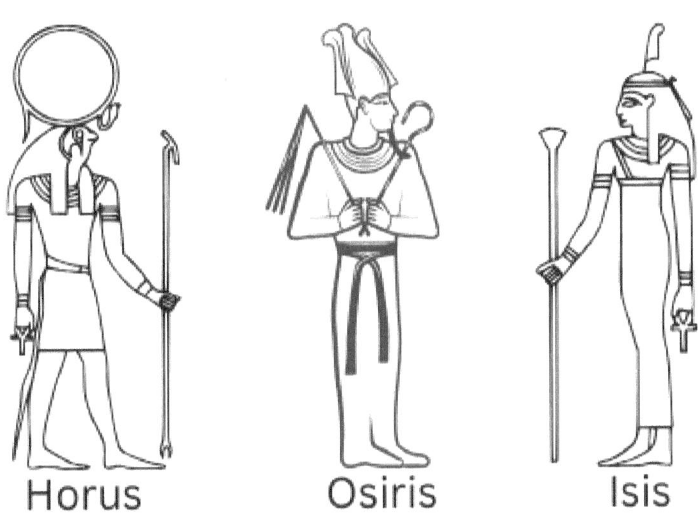

Jonathan Z. Smith, a University of Chicago scholar, wrote an article titled "Dying and Rising Gods" for the Encyclopedia of Religion in 1987, in which he states,

> "Osiris was murdered and his body dismembered and scattered. The pieces of his body were recovered and rejoined, and the god was rejuvenated. However, he did not return to his former mode of existence but rather journeyed to the underworld, where he became the powerful lord of the dead. In no sense can Osiris be said

10.   https://ancientegyptonline.co.uk/osiris/

11.   https://ancientegyptonline.co.uk/horus/

to have "risen" in the sense required by the dying and rising pattern; most certainly it was never conceived as an annual event. The repeated formula "Rise up, you have not died," whether applied to Osiris or a citizen of Egypt, signaled a new, permanent life in the realm of the dead. Osiris was considered to be the mythical prototype for the distinctive Egyptian process of mummification."[87]

Before Osiris, there was another Egyptian deity named Atum (the creator god), whose children were Shu (the god of dry air) and Tefnut (the goddess of moisture). Shu and Tefnut had children named Geb (earth) and Nut (sky). Geb and Nut had four children Isis, Osiris, Set, and Nephthys. See image below:

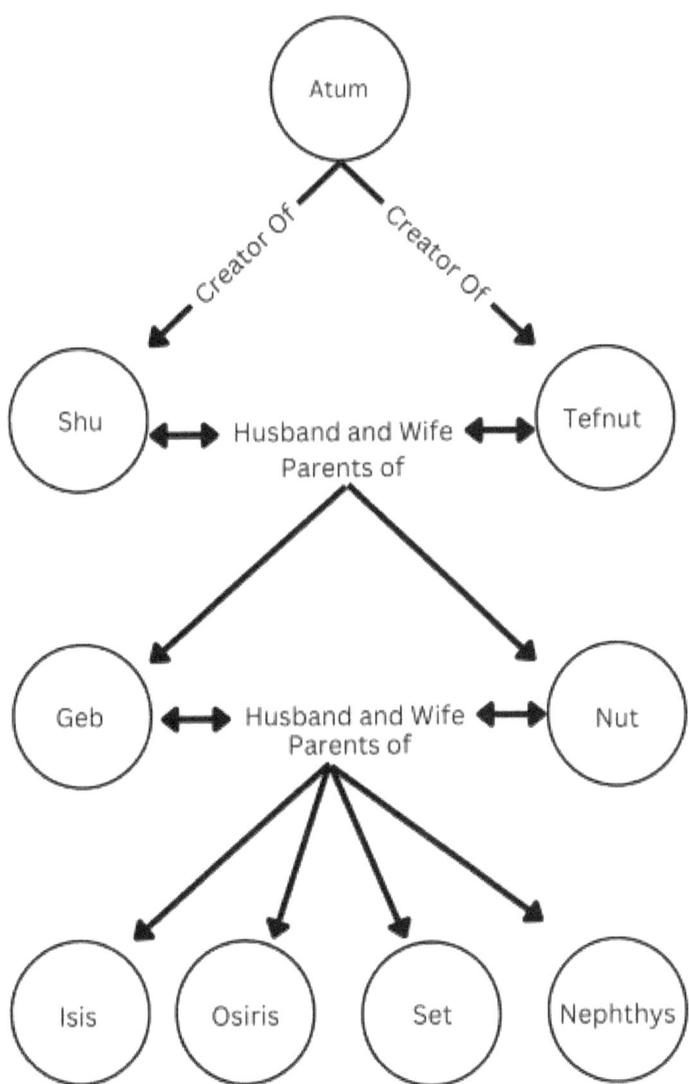

Family Tree of Isis, Osiris, and Horus

A few, of many, differences between Jesus and Osiris:

The Nature of Death and Resurrection:

● **Jesus:** Jesus' death by crucifixion is a singular event in history, followed by His resurrection three days later as a testament to His Divine Nature and victory over sin and death.

● **Osiris:** Osiris' brother Set murdered him, dismembered him, and dispersed his pieces all over Egypt. In a mythical story that represents the annual flooding and growth cycles of the Nile, his wife Isis put him back together and brought him back to life.

Role and Significance:

● **Jesus:** Considered the Son of God by Christians, Jesus' role is as a Savior who died for the sins of humanity and was resurrected, offering eternal life to believers.

● **Osiris:** Osiris is the god of the dead and the afterlife, symbolizing the cycle of life, death, and rebirth. He was also the judge of the deceased in the afterlife.

Worship and Rituals:

● **Jesus:** Worship of Jesus includes prayer, the sacraments (such as baptism and communion), and the celebration of religious holidays like Christmas and Easter.

● **Osiris:** Worship of Osiris involved complex burial rituals, mummification, and ceremonies like the Osiris Mysteries, which celebrated his death and resurrection to the underworld, not back to earth.

Upon closer examination, we see that Isis, Osiris, and Horus are three separate deities (one being a female) who do not share the same essence, which the Holy Trinity does. The only similarity between Isis, Osiris, Horus, and the Holy Trinity is the number three. There is no evidence from either biblical or non-biblical sources that suggests the number three is pagan. Therefore, it is safe to say that the claim that the Trinity is rooted in paganism is false due to a lack of evidence.

Asar, Aset, and Heru

Secular African American studies scholar Jennifer Williams writes[1] that North Africa birthed the mythologies concerning the gods who manifested themselves as three persons. Williams contends that one of the first trinity stories comes from ancient Kemet, which asserted that three deities – Asar, Aset, and Heru – were part of the same god, one of whom began life as a human. Scholars refer to this ancient trinity as the Asar-Aset-Heru trinity. Williams added that the roles and natures of the father and son (Asar and Heru) in the Asar-Aset-Heru trinity lay a foundation for the Christian Trinity doctrine—established many centuries later. There is absolutely zero evidence for this statement by her.

The triune deity in the mythology she used is just Isis, Osiris, and Horus, with the new names Asar, Aset, and Heru. The story of Asar (Osiris), Aset (Isis), and Heru (Horus) is one of the most famous and enduring myths in ancient Egyptian mythology. It is a tale of death, resurrection, and the struggle for power that symbolizes the eternal cycle of life, death, and rebirth. Here is a brief recap of their story along with further parts of it:

Asar (Osiris) - The King and God of the Underworld

Asar was a benevolent king of Egypt and the god of the afterlife, agriculture, and resurrection. He brought civilization to the people of Egypt, teaching them the arts of agriculture and orderly living. His brother, Set (Seth), grew jealous of his power and popularity. Set tricked Asar into lying in a beautifully decorated coffin, which he then sealed and threw into the Nile. Asar's coffin was carried away to the city of Byblos, where it became embedded in the trunk of a tree.

Aset (Isis) - The Goddess of Magic and Healing

Aset, the wife and sister of Asar, is one of the most prominent goddesses of ancient Egyptian religion. After Asar was murdered and

---

1. https://www.jstor.org/stable/24572921?mag=a-holy-trinity-in-ancient-egypt

Set hid his body away, Aset embarked on a long journey to find him. With her magic and determination, she discovered Asar's body encased within a tree in Byblos. She brought his body back to Egypt, but Set, upon discovering this, tore Asar's body into fourteen pieces and scattered them across Egypt.

Undeterred, Aset and her sister Nepthys searched for and reassembled the pieces of Asar's body. Using her magical powers, Aset resurrected Asar long enough for them to conceive their son, Heru. Asar then became the ruler of the underworld, a god of the dead and resurrection.

Heru (Horus) - The Falcon-headed God

Heru, the son of Asar and Aset, was raised in secret to protect him from Set. When Heru grew up, he challenged Set to avenge his father's death and claim his rightful throne. Their battle was long and hard-fought, with various tales describing the extensive struggles and trials Heru had to endure.

In one of the key battles, Set gouged out Heru's left eye, and Heru tore off one of Set's testicles. The eye of Heru, also known as the "Wadjet," became a powerful symbol of protection and sacrifice. Eventually, the gods intervened to stop the conflict and declared Heru the rightful ruler of Egypt, thus restoring order and uniting the Upper and Lower kingdoms.

Heru became associated with the living pharaoh, considered the earthly embodiment of the god. Asar's resurrection and Heru's victory over Set symbolized the triumph of order over chaos, and of life over death, reinforcing the themes of death, resurrection, and eternal life that were central to ancient Egyptian religion.

The myth of Asar, Aset, and Heru is a cornerstone of ancient Egyptian mythology, reflecting the values and beliefs of Egyptian culture regarding kingship, justice, and the afterlife.

A few, of many, differences between Jesus and Asar, Aset, Heru:

- **Nature of Divinity:** The Holy Trinity embodies the Christian monotheistic view of one God in three Persons, while Asar, Aset, and Heru are three distinct deities within a polytheistic framework.

- **Religious vs. Mythological Context:** The Trinity is a core theological doctrine in Christianity, whereas the trio of Asar, Aset, and Heru is part of mythological narratives explaining natural cycles and social orders.

- **Cultural Origins:** The Trinity originates from the Judeo-Christian tradition, deeply influencing Western religious thought, while the Egyptian trio comes from ancient Egyptian religion, reflecting its cosmology and societal values.

Yet again, the only similarities that stick out is number three. There is no evidence from either biblical or non-biblical sources that suggests the number three is pagan. Therefore, it is safe to say that the claim that the Trinity is rooted in paganism is false due to a lack of evidence.

Brahma, Vishnu, and Shiva

A triune deity dynamic is also present in Hinduism. The Sanskrit term Trimūrti, meaning "three forms," is assigned to the gods Brahma, Vishnu, and Shiva. These three divine personalities are said to be part of the same divine being, but this is modalism, not trinitarianism.

Brahma means "the creator"

Followers of Hinduism believe that Brahma made the world and all living things. Hindu legend says that Brahma was created from a lotus that grew out of Vishnu's navel while he was thinking about the empty seas of space. Then Brahma started to make things, including the universe and all the living things in it. Compared to Vishnu and Shiva, Brahma is not honored as much, even though he is the creator. One of the most well-known stories about Brahma is that he made the goddess Saraswati, who then came out of him and married him. It is said that she is the goddess of learning, arts, and knowledge.

Vishnu is the Protector

Vishnu is the one who keeps the world alive and safe. He is supposed to come back to earth when things are going badly in order to make things right between good and evil. Vishnu has taken on many forms, or avatars. Rama and Krishna are the most well-known. The reason these avatars are born is to fight bad forces that threaten the order of the universe. In his stories, Vishnu often shows how much he cares about people. He is usually shown lying on the snake Ananta, with Lakshmi, the goddess of wealth and cleanliness, at his feet.

Shiva: The Horrible One

Shiva is the god of change. He is known as "the breaker" because he causes death and damage. He is also the god of letting go of old habits. He plays a scary part, but he is also seen as a symbol of kindness. Shiva's ruin is not random; it is actually good because it makes room for good change and new things to be made. Shiva, one of the most loved gods in Hinduism, is also a figure of paradox because he lives in both a monastery and a house. His wife is Parvati, and their relationship is at the heart of many stories that talk about love, loyalty, and the balance of power. Ganesha, the elephant-headed god of knowledge and the removal of obstacles, and Kartikeya, the god of war, are both sons of Shiva.

How the three parts of the Trimurti are linked

There are many stories involving Shiva, Brahma, and Vishnu that show how their roles in keeping the world in balance are linked. Even though they do different things (creation, protection, and death), they work together to do other things. This repetitive process makes sure that the universe is always being made, preserved, and renewed. This is in line with the Hindu belief that the universe exists forever. The idea of the Trimurti shows how complicated the Hindu pantheon is. In this pantheon, gods represent different parts of life and the world, and creation and death are seen as connected processes that are needed to keep life going.

A few, of many, differences between Jesus and Brahma, Vishnu, and Shiva:

- **Nature of Divinity:** The Holy Trinity represents a single Divine essence in three Persons, while the Trimurti embodies three distinct deities with specific cosmic roles.

- **Unity vs. Function:** In Christianity, the Trinity emphasizes the unity of God's Nature, whereas Hinduism's Trimurti highlights the functional diversity in the universe's ongoing cycle.

- **Monotheism vs. Polytheism:** The foundational difference in belief systems—Christianity's monotheism contrasts sharply with the polytheistic framework of Hinduism.

- **Theological Context:** The Trinity is central to understanding Christian theology and God's relationship with humanity, while the Trimurti offers a framework for the cyclical nature of the universe in Hindu thought.

Once again, the only similarity that stands out is the third one being discussed here. It is not possible to find any proof, either from the Bible or from other sources, that the number three is associated with the pagan religion. It is thus reasonable to declare that the assertion that the Trinity has its origins in paganism is not true since there is insufficient evidence to support this claim.

Dharmakaya, Samdhogakaya, and Nirmanakaya

The concepts of Dharmakaya, Sambhogakaya, and Nirmanakaya are central to Mahayana Buddhism, particularly within Vajrayana (Tibetan Buddhism). These terms describe three aspects or "bodies" (kayas) of a Buddha, reflecting different dimensions of enlightenment. This trikaya doctrine offers a nuanced understanding of the Buddha's nature, illustrating how enlightened beings can exist and manifest across different realms of existence to benefit sentient beings. Here's a brief overview of each:

Dharmakaya: The Truth Body

- **Nature:** The Dharmakaya is the ultimate truth, the absolute reality that is beyond conceptualization or form. It represents the Buddha's omniscient mind, free from delusion, embodying enlightenment and the true nature of all phenomena.

- **Significance:** Being the foundation of the other two bodies, Dharmakaya is the embodiment of the Buddha's wisdom and the law of Dharma itself. It is formless and represents the unmanifested, transcendent aspect of Buddha.

- **Manifestation:** Since the Dharmakaya transcends physical form, ordinary beings cannot directly perceive it. It is experienced as the ultimate state of liberation and enlightenment.

Sambhogakaya: The Enjoyment Body

- **Nature:** The Sambhogakaya is the body of bliss or enjoyment, existing in pure realms accessible only to highly realized bodhisattvas. It is a manifestation of the Buddha's enlightenment in a form that engages in enjoyment of the Dharma.

- **Significance:** This aspect allows the Buddha to communicate with bodhisattvas through teachings and guidance. It represents an intermediate state where enlightened wisdom is expressed in forms perceivable by those on advanced spiritual paths.

- **Manifestation:** The Sambhogakaya is depicted as residing in celestial realms, adorned with magnificent ornaments symbolizing the Buddha's virtues. It is through this body that the Buddha transmits teachings to bodhisattvas across different realms.

Nirmanakaya: The Emanation Body

- **Nature:** The Nirmanakaya is the physical form that a Buddha takes in order to be approachable by common sentient beings. It is the emanation or manifestation body, through which the Buddha interacts with the world.

- **Significance:** This aspect of the Buddha's existence is crucial for the sake of sentient beings. It allows the Buddha to perform acts of compassion, teach the Dharma, and guide beings along the path to enlightenment.

- **Manifestation:** Historical figures such as Shakyamuni Buddha (Siddhartha Gautama) are considered

Nirmanakayas. These emanations can take various forms suited to the needs of beings in different times and places.

Interconnectedness of the Three Kayas

The trikaya doctrine illustrates the multifaceted nature of the Buddha's existence and the ways in which enlightened wisdom can manifest. It reflects the deep compassion of Buddhas to make the path to enlightenment accessible across different levels of understanding and existence. The Dharmakaya represents the ultimate reality and wisdom, the Sambhogakaya communicates this wisdom to advanced practitioners in pure realms, and the Nirmanakaya brings teachings and guidance to ordinary beings in the physical world.

This framework provides a comprehensive view of how Buddhas continue to influence and guide sentient beings toward enlightenment, showcasing the boundless and compassionate nature of their wisdom and actions.

A few, of many, differences between the Holy Trinity and Brahma, Vishnu, and Shiva:

- **Theistic vs. Non-theistic:** Christianity's theistic approach contrasts with Buddhism's non-theistic or trans-theistic perspectives.

- **Personal God vs. Enlightened State:** Christianity's personal, relational God contrasts with Buddhism's focus on achieving an enlightened state devoid of a personal god.

- **Eternal Unchangeability vs. Impermanence:** The Eternal Nature of the Trinity contrasts with the Buddhist emphasis on impermanence, even in the nature of enlightenment.

- **Salvation vs. Self-Enlightenment:** Christianity's focus on salvation through the Trinity contrasts with Buddhism's emphasis on personal enlightenment through practice and understanding.

- **Unity vs. Functional Diversity:** The unified essence of the Trinity contrasts with the functional and manifestational diversity of the three kayas.

Once again, the only simulator that stands out is number three. There is no empirical evidence from either biblical or non-biblical sources to support the claim that the number three has pagan origins. Thus, it can be confidently stated that the assertion linking the Trinity to paganism is unfounded, as there is little evidence to support it.

Assyrian Mythology

Assyrian mythology, deeply intertwined with the broader Mesopotamian mythology, encompasses the Assyrian Empire's myths, gods, and religious beliefs, which flourished in ancient Mesopotamia. This region, located in what is now Iraq, Syria, and parts of Turkey and Iran, was a cradle of civilization and home to a rich tapestry of deities and myths that influenced the Assyrians. Here is an overview of some key elements:

Pantheon of Gods

The Assyrians shared many gods with the broader Mesopotamian culture, with each city often having its own patron deity. Key deities include:

- **Ashur:** is the supreme god of the Assyrian pantheon, associated with war and the state. Ashur did not have a distinct mythology but was represented as a winged sun disk or as a figure within a disk, symbolizing divine kingship and protection.

- **Ishtar:** The goddess of love, war, and fertility, Ishtar was a complex deity who played a crucial role in Assyrian religion. She was known for her fierce temperament and was often depicted as a lioness or with lion symbols.

- **Enlil:** The god of air, wind, and storms, Enlil was considered a creator god and a leader of the pantheon in early Mesopotamian mythology. He played a key role in the cosmology and religious life of the region.

- **Anu:** The sky god, representing the heavens, Anu was seen as the father of the gods and a figure of authority in the divine realm.

Myths and Epic Tales

While many Assyrian myths had Sumerian roots, the Assyrians modified and expanded upon them. One of the most significant literary works is the Epic of Gilgamesh, a masterpiece of ancient literature that tells the story of Gilgamesh, a semi-divine king of Uruk, and his quest for immortality. This epic explores themes of friendship, the human condition, and the quest for eternal life.

Religious Practices and Beliefs

The Assyrians believed in an afterlife, although their views were not as elaborately developed as those in ancient Egyptian religion. They conducted elaborate rituals to appease the gods, including animal sacrifices and temple ceremonies. Priests played a significant role in Assyrian society, acting as intermediaries between the gods and the people.

Cosmology and Creation Myths

The Assyrian creation myth, closely related to the Babylonian "Enuma Elish," describes the origins of the world from primordial chaos and the battle between the god Marduk (later associated with Ashur in Assyria) and the chaos monster Tiamat. Marduk's victory established order in the universe and led to the creation of humanity for the service of the gods.

Influence and Legacy

Assyrian mythology has left a lasting legacy on the cultures and religions that followed in the region. Its myths, gods, and religious practices influenced later civilizations, including the Babylonians and the Persians, and contributed to the rich tapestry of Middle Eastern cultural and religious history.

The stories and deities of Assyrian mythology, with their rich symbolism and deep connection to the natural and divine worlds, offer valuable insights into the beliefs, values, and daily life of the ancient Assyrians.

A few, of many, differences between the Holy Trinity and Assyrian Mythology:

- **Monotheism vs. Polytheism:** The unity of God in Christianity contrasts with the multiple deities of Assyrian mythology.

- **Unchanging God vs. Anthropomorphic Gods:** The immutable nature of the Christian God contrasts with the more human-like, changeable gods of Assyrian beliefs.

- **Salvation vs. Favor:** Christianity's focus on eternal salvation through faith contrasts with the Assyrian emphasis on immediate, worldly favor and protection from their gods.

- **Personal Relationship vs. Transactional Worship:** The personal and loving relationship with God promoted in Christianity contrasts with the more transactional nature of worship in Assyrian religion, where rituals and sacrifices were performed to gain favor or avert the wrath of the gods.

Once more, the number three is the only thing that stands out. There is no real proof from the Bible or other sources to back the idea that number three comes from pagan practices. So, we can say with certainty that the claim that the Trinity is connected to paganism is not true, since there is not much proof to back it up.

Nimrod, Semiramis and Tammuz

The story of Nimrod, Semiramis, and Tammuz is often cited in various historical, religious, and mythological contexts, but it's important to note that much of the narrative connecting these three figures directly is not found in ancient texts but rather in later interpretations and folklore. Here's an overview based on these later sources and interpretations:

Nimrod

Nimrod is a biblical figure mentioned in the Book of Genesis as a mighty hunter and a king of Shinar. He is often associated with the Tower of Babel story, which represents human pride and defiance against God. In historical and mythological interpretations, Nimrod is sometimes considered a symbol of rebellion and the establishment of powerful empires that stand in opposition to Divine will.

Semiramis

Semiramis is a legendary figure and is said to have been an Assyrian queen. Her story is a blend of historical fact and myth, with ancient historians like Herodotus and Ctesias providing differing accounts of her life. Over time, Semiramis became associated with tales of remarkable beauty, cunning, and ambition. She is often depicted as a powerful ruler who expanded her empire and built magnificent cities, including Babylon.

Tammuz

Tammuz is an ancient Mesopotamian god associated with fertility, agriculture, and the cycle of life and death. The worship of Tammuz included annual mourning rituals, reflecting the seasonal cycle of growth in the spring and death in the summer. His myth includes themes of death, descent into the underworld, and resurrection, reflecting the agricultural cycle of sowing, growth, and harvest.

The Interconnected Tale

• In later interpretations and folklore, these three figures are sometimes woven into a single narrative that reflects themes of power, divinity, and mortality. According to some versions of the tale:

• Nimrod marries Semiramis, and they have a son, Tammuz.

Semiramis declares herself to be the goddess Ishtar (the Akkadian counterpart of Inanna) and Nimrod to be a god, and Tammuz as a divine being, linking their rule to the divine.

• After Nimrod's death, Semiramis claims that he has ascended to the sun and has become a sun god. Tammuz, associated with vegetation and fertility, dies but is miraculously resurrected, reinforcing the cycle of death and rebirth.

It's important to emphasize that this interconnected tale of Nimrod, Semiramis, and Tammuz as a family is not found in ancient texts but rather is a synthesis of later interpretations, folklore, and speculation. The actual historical and mythological records about these figures are separate and belong to different contexts and time periods. The blending of their stories reflects an attempt to unify various mythological and historical strands into a coherent narrative that explains complex themes of power, divinity, and the natural world.

A few, among many, differences between the Holy Trinity and Nimrod, Semiramis, and Tammuz:

• **Theological Focus:** The Holy Trinity embodies the depth of Christian theological reflection on God's Nature and interactions with humanity, while the narratives of

Nimrod, Semiramis, and Tammuz are more focused on earthly rule, cultural achievements, and the natural cycles, viewed through a mythological lens.

● **Divinity vs. Humanity:** The Holy Trinity represents a unique understanding of Divine unity and diversity, whereas Nimrod and Semiramis are primarily seen as human (or deified human) figures and Tammuz as a deity within a polytheistic context.

● **Salvation and Eternal Life:** Christian teachings on the Trinity are deeply intertwined with themes of salvation, redemption, and eternal life, contrasting with the more temporal and cyclical concerns seen in the stories of Nimrod, Semiramis, and Tammuz.

● **Immutable Divinity vs. Mythological Evolution:** The nature of God in Christianity is characterized by immutability and eternity, contrasting with the more dynamic and anthropomorphic depictions of Nimrod, Semiramis, and Tammuz, whose stories and significance have evolved over time.

Once again, just the number three sticks out. No evidence from the Bible or other sources supports the claim that number three stems from pagan customs. So, we can state with certainty that the argument that the Trinity is linked to paganism is false, as there is little evidence to support it. No factual evidence from biblical or non-biblical sources supports the assertion that the number three has pagan origins. Thus, the statement relating the Trinity to paganism is baseless, as there is insufficient evidence to back it up.

Trinity Teaching in Christianity

The Trinity in Christianity is set apart from other teachings in that it hinges on the well-documented life of an actual historical figure (not a fabricated, exaggerated story of a figure like Nimrod). The resurrection of Jesus, which is the centerpiece of the Christian Trinity doctrine, is not just claimed in writings, it was affirmed by more than 500 eyewitnesses and by thousands more who were willing to die for what they knew to be true in the decades following the crucifixion.

Multiple scriptures also substantiate the Christian Trinity teaching, and the integrity of Scripture can be empirically validated via an analysis of biblical prophecy. There are more than 1,000 Bible prophecies in Scripture, and more than 90% of them have been fulfilled by this point in history. If just one of these prophecies can be proven false, the claimed inerrancy of the Bible, and the integrity of the Trinity doctrine, will be undermined.

No Bible prophecies have been proven inaccurate, partially accurate, or an outright error. Bible prophecy has been scrutinized by skeptics and believers. Though not all agree on what this means, all agree that the accuracy rate of Bible prophecy, including prophecies regarding the crucifixion and resurrection, is 100%. The statistical probability of this happening, without Divine, supernatural intervention, is zero. This sets the biblical narrative, and the Christian Trinity doctrine, apart from all other teachings.

That is not a spiritual statement, it is a mathematical statement. Josh McDowell wrote[88] that Jesus fulfilled more than 125 prophecies when He walked the Earth approximately 2000 years ago.

The statistical probability of Jesus fulfilling even less than half of those prophecies is one in 10 to the 129th power. That number is staggering—virtually unimaginable. It approximates the number of atoms, not in our solar system, not in our galaxy, but in the universe.

One in 10 to the 129th power is statistically zero. That is, the mathematical probability of Jesus fulfilling less than half of the Messianic prophecies attributed to Him is statistically zero.

Bible prophecy verifies the supernatural (or inspired) nature of Scripture, which in turn verifies the integrity of the Christian Trinity doctrine since the doctrine is based on Scripture.

Do some of the written mythologies noted in this chapter predate the formalization of the Christian Trinity doctrine? Yes. *However, Old Testament writings serve as the foundation for Christian theology, and Christians believe the foundation for the Trinity doctrine is present in the Old Testament.*

Christians note that Jesus said that He did not come to abolish the Law, but to fulfill it.[89] This means the New Testament seamlessly builds upon, amplifies, and clarifies the Old Testament—it does not erase or contradict the inspired writings of Moses or the prophets.

Christians also believe that before the widespread use of written language, the truth of God (later to be captured in the writing that would become the Bible) was known by all and shared via oral tradition. Before quickly discounting the accuracy of oral storytelling, Scientific America reported[90] that linguists and geographers have studied 18 Aboriginal stories and determined they maintained an exceptional degree of integrity over 400 generations. And in 1985, a Royal Commission on Aboriginal Peoples report[91] led the Canadian High Court to rule that Indigenous Oral Histories were accurate and admissible in court.

Scientists have verified that oral traditions can be as accurate as written histories. At first, spiritual oral traditions were carefully maintained and accurate, but in time, the stories were corrupted with the spread of sin. Satan encouraged them to develop into mythologies and anti-religions in order to undermine, deceive, and discourage people from following God's truth.

Nevertheless, Christians believe that correct oral traditions concerning Creation, the Flood, and the Nature of God precede all false religions and teachings. What is now viewed as the Old Testament presents the true record, as originally expressed and passed on via oral accounts.

Christians believe that, although the word Trinity is not found in the Bible, Old Testament era Jews believed that God is "One" (see Deuteronomy 6:4) and yet at the same time, believed He is more than One. This is reflected in the Midrash, the Talmud, and in Old Testament references to God as being plural. A few examples follow:

- "Elohim" references God in Genesis 1:1. The term is plural.
- "Us" references God in Isaiah 6:8. The term is plural.
- "Maker" references God in Isaiah 54:5. The term is plural.

Jews in the Old Testament were aware of God's multifaceted Nature. In New Testament times, through progressive revelation, God revealed His Triune Nature—expressed in human terms as The Father, the Son, and the Holy Spirit. The Godhead, the theological term for the Nature of God, indicates that God is three, yet One—all aspects of God are more than One in purpose, they are One in essence.

Multiple Scriptures point to the Trinity. The Bible notes:

- There is only one uncreated, eternal, true God (Ex. 3:14; Deut. 6:4; John 17:3).

• There will never be any other uncreated, eternal, true God(s) (Isaiah 43:10; 44:6-8; 1 Cor. 8:4-6; Gal. 4:8).

However, the Bible also notes:

• The "Father is God" (1 Cor. 8:4-6; 2 Peter 1:17).
• Jesus is God (John 1:1-3; Col. 1:16).
• And the Holy Spirit is God (Job 33:4; Acts 5:3-4; 1 Cor. 2:11).

Further, Scripture presents the Son and the Holy Spirit as having uniquely Divine attributes that link themselves to God. The following verses do not just associate Jesus and the Spirit with God; they affirm that Jesus and the Spirit *are* God:

Jesus is presented as God in that He is:

• Creator in John 1:3: 1 Cor. 8:6: Col 1:16-17 Heb. 1:2: Rev. 3:14.

• Eternal in John 1:1, 8:58, 17:5; Col. 1:17; Heb. 1:2.

• Savior in 1 John 4:4: Acts 5:31; Phil. 2:22, 3:20; Rom. 5:1.

• Omniscient in John 16:30.

• Omnipresent in Matt. 18:20, 28:20; John 3:13; Eph. 1:23, 4:10; Col. 3:11.

Similarly, the Holy Spirit is presented as God as He is:

• Eternal in Heb. 9:14.
• Omniscient in 1 Cor. 2:10-11.
• Omnipresent in Psa. 139:7.
• Savior in Rom. 8:1-27.

The dual Nature (Divine and human) of Jesus Christ is called the Hypostatic Union (communicatio idiomatum, Latin for "communication of properties"). The Hypostatic Union teaching notes that Jesus simultaneously manifested human and Divine attributes. This means that the man Jesus could lay claim to the glory He had with the Father before the world was made (John 17:5), claim that He descended from heaven (John 3:13), claim omnipresence (Matt. 28:20), and claim He had the authority and power to lay down His life and raise it up again (a key point in the Trinity doctrine).

The Divinity of Christ and the Triune Nature of God were noted in New Testament writings and affirmed by the early leaders of the New Testament Church before being formally constituted into a doctrine at the Council of Nicaea in 325 A.D. Some early references to the Trinity include:

- **Justin Martyr (100–165):** "And that Christ being Lord, and God the Son of God...He is called the begotten Word of God, is even God...He is God..." [92]

- **Irenaeus of Lyons (d. c. 202):** "It is proper, then, that I should begin with the first and most important head, that is, God the Creator, who made the heaven and the earth, and all things that are therein . . . and to demonstrate that there is nothing either above Him or after Him; nor that, influenced by anyone, Lord, the only Creator, the only Father, alone containing all things, and Himself commanding all things into existence." [93]

- **Tertullian:** "Thus Christ is Spirit of Spirit, and God of God, as light of light is kindled... That which has come forth out of God is at once God and the Son of God...He is Spirit of Spirit and God of God... This ray of God, then, as it was always foretold in ancient times, descending into a certain virgin, and made flesh in her womb, is in His birth God and man united."[94]

o **Tertullian:** "The Father is God, and the Son is God, and the Holy Ghost is God, and each is God..." [95]

The Trinity doctrine was formalized after much prayer and debate at the Council of Nicaea in the early fourth century. The Creed was established in response to attacks on the truth, and to note that the Christian Church believes what has been evident from the beginning of time. God is One, yet more.

The truth has not changed but was revealed in more clarity in God's perfect way and time. The early Creed read:

"We believe in one God, the Father almighty, Maker of heaven and earth,
and of all things visible and invisible.
And in one Lord Jesus Christ, the Son of God, the
only-begotten,
begotten of the Father before all ages.
Light of Light, true God of true God, begotten not made,
of one essence with the Father by whom all things were made;
who for us men and for our salvation, came down from heaven,
and was incarnate of the Holy Spirit and the Virgin Mary
and became man.
And He was crucified for us under Pontius Pilate,
and suffered, and was buried.
And the third day He rose again, according to the Scriptures;

**and ascended into heaven, and sits at the right hand of the
Father;
and He shall come again with glory to judge the living and the
dead;
whose Kingdom shall have no end.
And in the Holy Spirit"**

Church leaders at the Council of Nicaea (see Chapter 8) did not invent the Trinity doctrine, or plagiarize the concept from various mythologies. They simply affirmed, clarified, and formalized the teachings advanced by biblical writers, together with the oral traditions which had predated written language.

The Christian Trinity doctrine stands apart from lesser trinity concepts found in various mythologies because it is substantiated by Scripture (which has been validated by historians, archeologists, manuscript experts, and Bible prophecy scholars), and has Jesus as its centerpiece: *an actual historical figure whose life, crucifixion, and resurrection are exceptionally well documented.*

Chapter 10: The Multiverse and the Multidimensional Nature of God

This chapter touches on an interesting dynamic in academia today. Most scholars who specialize in the higher sciences readily accept the idea of a multiverse. Our universe may have unique dynamics, but it's not unique. Multiverse theorists hold that there can be multiple, parallel, or alternate universes and that it is possible to bridge the boundaries separating these planes or realities, thus simultaneously existing in different forms (note: the famous "double slit experiment" [see below] proved at least some aspects of this hypothesis are possible).

Some may consider the thought to be wild— marked more by fantasy, than facts. However, it is worth noting that the view is held by recent notables, such as Lee Smolin, Don Page, Brian Greene, Max Tegmark, Alan Guth, Andrei Linde, Michio Kaku, David Deutsch, Leonard Susskind, Alexander Vilenkin, Yasunori Nomura, Raj Pathria, Laura Mersini-Houghton, Neil deGrasse Tyson, Sean Carroll, and Stephen Hawking— all highly respected in the field of quantum physics.

The question is, if science accepts the idea of multiple planes of existence and that at least some aspects of creation within one dimension can theoretically crossover and manifest themselves into another plane, then why does higher science almost categorically reject the idea of a multidimensional God—a Being Who exists outside of our dimension, or reality, but is also intimately invested in the workings *of our reality?*

This chapter notes that, though some of the language is different, the Bible supports the concept of a multiverse, and that the concept of a multiverse supports the concept of the Trinity.

The thought that there is much more to creation than what we can see is not new. Greek philosophers wrote of this centuries before the birth of Christ. Late Renaissance period leaders in science echoed the thought.

With a specialty in mathematics and quantum physics, Fatima Zahra, PhD (School of Electro-Mechanical Engineering, Xidian University, Xi'an, China) looks more closely at how the idea of the multiverse perspective might seem more realistic to us once we come to understand the terms and conditions she writes about below. In quite simplistic language for such a complicated subject, Dr. Zahra concisely explains:

Introduction to Dimensions

The word "dimension" originates from the Latin word *dimensio*, which means "measured out." A dimension is a parameter or measure of an object's geometric properties. Dimension is the general term for the measurement of an object's size, such as a box, and it is typically expressed as height, width, and length. The number of independent directions in which an object can be moved directly correlates with its dimension.

Historical Development of Dimensional Theory

Ancient people learned geometric abilities by visiting Egypt and Babylon, where they learned lengths, angles, areas, and sizes to address everyday difficulties such as building structures, keeping track of the stars, and crafting. For the first time in history, it was utilized by the Egyptians and the Babylonians for surveying and estimating the pyramids' measurements (Four-Dimensional Geometry, 2024).

Euclid is the first and one of history's most remarkable names known for dimensional geometry. He invented the method of using deduction from first principles and is recognized as the father of dimensional geometry. The concept of fractional dimension was first developed by German mathematician Felix Hausdorff in 1918 (James Dow Allen, 2016). This idea has been very beneficial, particularly in the hands of French-Polish mathematician Benoit Mandelbrot, who popularized the term "fractal" and demonstrated the potential applications of fractional dimensions in many areas of practical mathematics. Mathematicians constantly broaden the field by contributing their time and life's work to improve our understanding of what the fourth dimension is and how its geometry functions (Massopust, 2016).

The new generation knows about higher dimensions, but they never fully get them. It is important to realize that it took a long time for people to figure out what higher dimensions are all about. In the past, it was hard to even think about them because they did not have the right ideas. It took a lot of time and effort to understand the math behind the higher dimensions.

Importance of Understanding Dimensions

One basic idea that is essential to mathematics, physics, and other disciplines is the concept of dimension. The quantity of independent parameters or coordinates needed to specify a point in a system or space is referred to by this term. In geometry, the term "dimension" was first utilized to describe the characteristics of geometric objects, such as points, lines, and planes. In many domains, the idea has become indispensable for explaining a broad variety of occurrences as it has developed over time.

Practical Applications of Dimensional Concepts

Dimension in Mathematics and Physics:

In mathematics and physics, dimension refers to the smallest number of coordinates required to uniquely identify any point within a given space or object. Cartesian coordinates are used to describe physical space by using the three integers x, y, and z. These are used to specify a point's position about three perpendicular axes. Such as the length, width, and height are represented by the x, y, and z axes, respectively. We can find the location of any point in physical space by giving the values of x, y, and z. The properties of many different objects and systems, such as geometric shapes, vector spaces, and abstract systems, are described by the mathematical concept of dimension by defining the coordinate position of a point. For example, a line has one dimension because only one coordinate is needed to specify a point on it; a circle is a two-dimensional geometric object because two coordinates are needed.

Space and dimension are strongly associated concepts. Space is a basic notion in physics that describes the three-dimensional expanse of objects and events. 3D-space is the term used to describe this three-dimensional space. The three dimensions of actual space are not the only dimensions that have been added to the concept of space. In reality, some physics theories suggest that there might be more dimensions than the four that we typically perceive, such as extra-spatial and time-like dimensions.

Dimension in Engineering Design:

In engineering, "dimension" refers to the process of defining a design object's physical characteristics to give detailed information about its shape, location, and size. This critical stage for the manufacturing and assembly teams removes the need for guesswork to attain the required precision by providing clear and concise information. In the field of engineering, it is crucial for the creation of technical drawings, models, and blueprints. The dimensioning process facilitates effective communication of design intents. Depending on the requirements of the design, a variety of dimensioning techniques are employed, from simpler ones like linear and angular to more intricate ones like chain and baseline dimensioning.

Dimension in Art and Literature:

Art objects are restricted by the dimensions of space and time due to the limitations of nature. Because of this, art items can be divided into three categories: art that has two dimensions, art that has three dimensions, or art that has four dimensions. Divisions within each category are essentially the result of variations in the materials and methods employed (Forsythe et al., 2011). Art pieces have typically been easily classified into a clear category throughout history. However, in order to determine whether the categories they fell into were arbitrary or real, artists started experimenting with the limits of new materials in the nineteenth century. Two-dimensional art is created on flat surfaces like paper, canvas, or even cave walls. The three primary categories of this art are painting, printing, and drawing. All two-dimensional art was produced on a flat surface (Forsythe et al., 2011).

Beyond the flat surface, three-dimensional art includes depth, width, and height. Three-dimensional art is created using four primary techniques. All forms of three-dimensional art employ one or more of the following four techniques: casting, modeling, carving, or assembling. Installation is a type of three-dimensional art that first appeared in the 20th century. In an installation, the observer is either completely encircled by the artist's altered space or they can move around it.

New media art, performance, video, and projection mapping are all included in the relatively new category of four-dimensional art, sometimes known as time-based art. In order to make an image fit the surface of the item it is projected onto, one or more two- or three-dimensional objects, typically buildings, are spatially mapped into a virtual program. Modern art explores spaces that go beyond just three dimensions.

Types of Dimensions

235

One Dimensional:

For a one-dimensional figure, just one measurement is feasible. An illustration of a one-dimensional object is a line segment drawn on a surface. In a one-dimension figure, only length is measured, not width. There is only one value required to specify a point on the line, and that is the length.

Two Dimensional:

In geometry, two-dimensional shapes or objects are flat planar figures with lengths and widths. Two-dimensional shapes can only be measured in two planes which have no thickness. Different examples of two-dimensional objects include triangles, squares, circles, and rectangles. Figures can be categorized according to their dimensions, usually length by width.

Three Dimensional:

A solid shape, often known as a three-dimensional object, is anything that occupies space. The fact that everything has three dimensions—length, width, and height—justifies the term "three-dimensional." The following are a few examples of solid shapes: spheres, hemispheres, prisms, cones, pyramids, cubes, and cuboids.

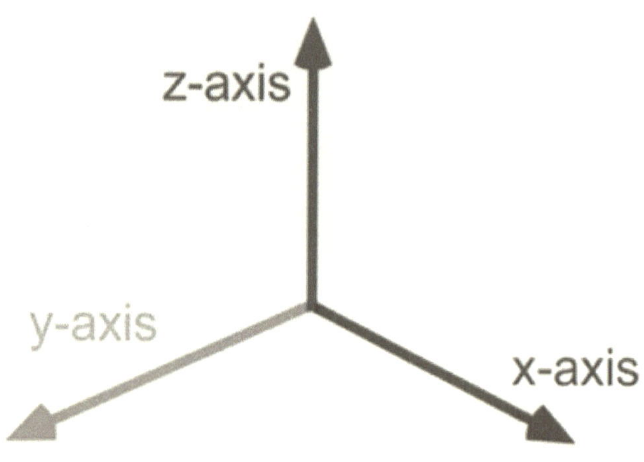

We can visualize the whole universe as a three-dimensional cube with three spatial axes representing length, width, and height as they move left and right, up and down, and forward and backward along time, which is a dimension that is perceived but not directly observed. In a strictly mathematical sense, the axes of data in a cartesian system, often consisting of an x-, y-, and z-axis represent the number of dimensions.

Four Dimensions:

Applications in Math:

Understanding four-dimensional spaces and other higher-dimensional spaces is essential to mathematics, especially geometry. Visualizing these areas complicates our traditional three-dimensional thinking, but they also enhance problem-solving abilities. Mathematicians can investigate these abstract spaces with the help of ideas like hypercubes. The fourth dimension in geometry is essential to visual representation. It goes beyond what we normally encounter and tests our comprehension of intricate spatial patterns. Even though four-dimensional space is not directly visible to us, arithmetic may help us grasp and express it, which broadens our understanding of geometry.

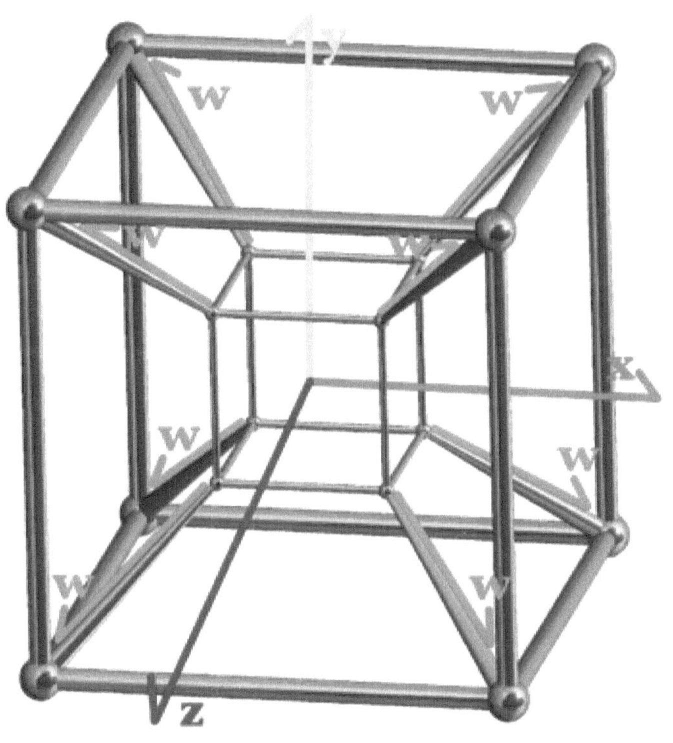
W
W
W
W
Y
X
W
W
W
W
Z

Applications in Physics:

The foundation of our understanding of physical rules and predictions in physics is the fourth dimension, which is represented by time in space-time. This idea is fundamental to modern physics theories such as Einstein's general relativity. Time must be added as a fourth dimension in order to make precise predictions about how things will behave. In the framework of general relativity, time's appearance as the fourth dimension is essential for transforming our conception of gravity. It defines gravity as the profoundly interwoven fourth dimension caused by big objects curving space-time. In this situation, ignoring time would make it extremely difficult to explain gravitational events.

Four Dimensions in Art:

The fourth dimension is defined differently in other fields. The life of the mind is a common conception of the fourth dimension among writers and artists. The fourth dimension is metaphysical in the eyes of others. We can examine more closely what makes three dimensions three-dimensional and then extrapolate what a fourth dimension might be based on these concepts to gain a better understanding of what a fourth dimension might be like.

Our observable world has three dimensions: length, width, and height. Our senses of hearing and vision, for example, provide us with empirical evidence that allows us to observe these dimensions. In our three dimensional space, we may find the locations of points and the directions of vectors along a reference point. A tesseract is a four-dimensional analog of a cube. It is a hypercube that exists in four spatial dimensions, with each side being a cube. While we can conceptually define and study tesseracts, it is extremely difficult to directly visualize or observe them, just as a two-dimensional being would struggle to comprehend three dimensions.

The progression from a 2D square to a 3D cube provides a helpful analogy for understanding the leap to 4D objects. A 2D square has four points, four lines, and four sides, while a 3D cube has eight points, twelve lines, and six square faces. Following this pattern, a 4D tesseract would have sixteen points, thirty-two lines, twenty-four square faces, and eight cube faces. Comparing 2D and 3D photographs is a useful way to gain some intuition about the difference between three and four dimensions. However, it is important to remember that the actual experience of a fourth spatial dimension would be radically different from anything we can directly perceive or imagine.

Visualization of Higher Dimensions:

Consider a notepad as an example, which has three dimensions. It has three dimensions: depth, width, and height. If we elevate that notepad above a level surface and illuminate it with a light source. The shadow cast by the notebook is two-dimensional, or 2-D. It just has width and height. Thus, the 3-D notebook cannot be directly seen in that shadow. However, examining the 2-D shadow of the notebook from various angles can provide details on the third dimension of the book.

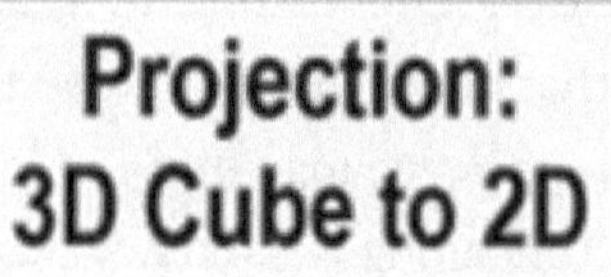

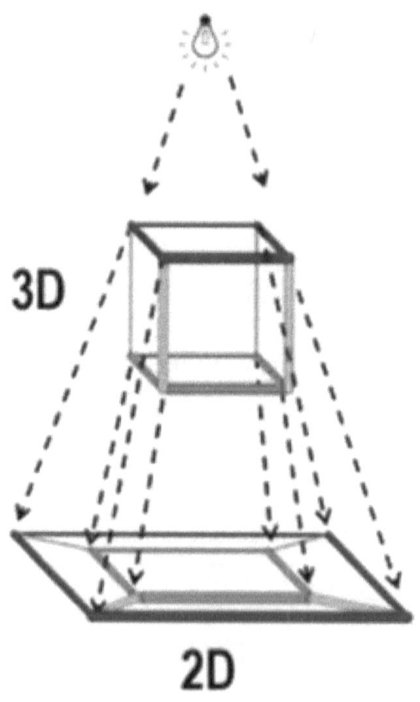

4D Shadow: Due to the fact that items in two dimensions are shadowed by three-dimensional entities, scientists have hypothesized that objects in four dimensions would also produce a three-dimensional shadow. That is why, even if we are unable to directly witness four dimensions, we can yet perceive this "shadow" in our three spatial dimensions. It is a four-dimensional shadow (Peltonen, 2023).

Similar to how Oklahoma State University mathematician Henry Segerman produced and documented his own four-dimensional sculptures. Using rings, he has constructed dodecadodecahedron-shaped structures, 120 dodecahedra being a three-dimensional shape with 12 pentagonal faces. Although an ant on a piece of paper can only see in two dimensions, this does not rule out the existence of a third dimension. It simply means that the ant can only perceive two dimensions directly and that it must use logic to deduce a third dimension from the two it can see. In a similar vein, people can conjecture about the nature of the fourth dimensions without actually experiencing them (Zamboj, 2018).

Differences between 3D and 4D Images:

The four-dimensional cube tesseract exemplifies how the three-dimensional world defined by x, y, and z can expand into a fourth dimension. Using a four-dimensional vector that incorporates additional variables like w, mathematicians, physicists, and other scientists and researchers can represent vectors in the fourth dimension (Preeti Juturu, 2016).

Four-dimensional figures known as 4-polytopes are among the more intricately shaped objects in the fourth dimension. These items demonstrate how 3D and 4D images differ from one another. The term "fourth dimension" has been used by some experts to refer to the inclusion of effects on media formats beyond the three dimensions' capabilities. According to Preeti Juturu (2016), this includes "four-dimensional movies" that modify the movie theater's setting through changes in motion, temperature, humidity, and other factors that can create an immersive experience similar to that of a virtual reality simulation. The term "fourth dimension" is also occasionally used by ultrasonographers who specialize in studying three-dimensional ultrasonography to describe ultrasonography that has a time-dependent component, such as a live recording. These techniques rely on the fourth dimension of time. Consequently, they fail to consider the fourth spatial dimension that tesseracts attempt to represent.

Different Dimensions:

Scientists think there might be many more dimensions beyond these three that are currently apparent. In actuality, the ten dimensions of the universe are proposed by the Superstring Theory theoretical framework. The fundamental forces of existence, the universe, and all of its component particles are all governed by these various features.

There are three dimensions in space length, width, and depth and one dimension in time in the world as we know "that start with the same initial condition as this one (occurring with) the Big Bang." However, there's always the surreal chance that there are a ton more dimensions out there. One of the most influential physics models of the past fifty years, string theory, holds that there are ten dimensions in which the universe works. However, that raises the important question, which is: If there are ten dimensions, why aren't we experiencing them all? Those dimensions may be so small and transient that we are unable to notice them at this time (Active Inference, 2022).

When someone refers to "different dimensions," we usually picture alternate worlds or parallel universes that exist alongside our own but have distinct laws of physics or histories. But this common portrayal of dimensions is actually very different from the reality of them and how they function in the ordering of our universe.

Dimensions are just the various aspects of what we understand to be reality, to put it simply. The three dimensions that are the x, y, and z axes, respectively, that characterize the length, width, and depth of every object in our universes are instantly apparent to us (Williams, 2014).

Superstring Theory states that the concept of potential universes originates in the fifth and sixth dimensions. We would be able to gauge the similarities and differences between our world and other plausible ones if we could see into the fifth dimension, where we would see a world that is marginally different from our own.

In the sixth, all of the potential universes that begin with the same beginning conditions as the Big Bang would be compared and positioned on a plane of conceivable worlds. Theoretically, we could travel to different futures or back in time if we could grasp the fifth and sixth dimensions (Williams, 2014).

The universes that could exist with various starting conditions are accessible to us in the seventh dimension. Here, everything has changed from the beginning of time, in contrast to the fifth and sixth cases where the starting conditions were the same and the actions that followed were different. Another plane of such potential world histories is provided by the eighth dimension; these histories start with distinct initial conditions and branch out indefinitely (Active Inference, 2022).

We can compare every conceivable universe history in the ninth dimension, beginning with any possible combination of physics rules and initial conditions. We reach the point where everything imaginable and feasible is covered in the tenth and last dimension. It is the natural boundary of our horizons, beyond which we, as lowly creatures, are incapable of imagining anything (Rigollet & Hütter, 2023).

Challenges in Understanding Higher Dimensions:

These higher-dimensional spaces are more difficult to visualize because they go beyond what we normally experience, but they are crucial to solving different issues and analyzing complex structures.

Edwin A. Abbott illustrated the issue of experiencing dimensions other than your own in a novella he published in 1884. According to Abbot's "Flatland: A Romance of Many Dimensions," a square lives in a two-dimensional world. When a square lives in two dimensions, it is surrounded by rectangles, triangles, and circles, but it can only perceive other lines. A sphere visits the square one day. When the sphere explains 3D items to the square, at first glance, all it appears to be is a circle, and the square is unable to understand what the sphere means.

The square eventually understands when the sphere introduces it to the 3D universe. He perceives complete, three-dimensional shapes rather than just lines. The square, full of confidence, asks the sphere, to its surprise, what is out there in the 3D world. The sphere signifies the reader because it is incapable of understanding a world larger than this one. Because our brains are not wired to perceive anything beyond our immediate environment, it will probably require a glimpse from another reality for us to comprehend.

How does this relate to God? The Significance of Understanding God in Different Dimensions:

From our 3D perspective, higher dimensional spaces and objects would seem "impossible." In the same way that a 2D creature would be taken aback by the sight of a 3D cube, we would probably react profoundly almost mystically when we saw 4D occurrences. This feeling of the "impossible" is frequently connected to how people see God.

The nature of God is often described in spiritual teachings as existing in higher dimensions beyond our perception. Concepts like infinite awareness, omniscience, and perfection of physical laws are related with higher dimensional authenticities. Our brains and sensory organs are fundamentally limited to 3D space and 1D time. Trying to directly experience or visualize higher dimensions is similar to a 2D being trying to understand our 3D world; it is simply beyond our distinctive thinking and perceptual abilities.

The comparison of Flatland, a two-dimensional universe where entities may only move left, right, forward, or backward, can help us recognize how God might observe the world from a higher level. The idea that God must have two time dimensions in order to be able to hear and respond to different people simultaneously is another aspect of this concept. The idea of God existing in a higher dimension is often linked to the idea of omnipresence, where God is supposed to be present everywhere at the same time. This idea is often used to explain how God can be both superior and inherent, existing beyond the physical world while still being present within it.

References for Dr. Zahra's section above include:

History of Thought: Four Dimensional Geometry. (2024). Brown.edu. Massopust, P. R. (2016). Dimension theory. Elsevier EBooks, 101–127.

James Dow Allen. (2016). The 200 greatest mathematicians. Fabpedigree.com.

Rigollet, P., & Hütter, J.-C. (2023). High-dimensional statistics. ArXiv.org.

Zamboj, M. (2018). Sections and Shadows of Four-Dimensional Objects. Nexus Network Journal/Nexus Network Journal, 20(2), 475–487.

Williams, M. (2014, December 11). A universe of 10 dimensions. Phys.org; Phys.org.

Preeti Juturu. (2016, October 12). What are Dimensions? Vectors, The Fourth-Dimension, and More Medium; Medium.

Peltonen, K., & Luotoniemi, T. (Eds.). (2023). Shapes in Action. Aalto korkeakoulusäätiö.

Forsythe, A., Nadal, M., Sheehy, N., Cela-Conde, C. J., & Sawey, M. (2011). Predicting beauty: Fractal dimension and visual complexity in art. British Journal of Psychology, 102(1), 49–70.

About 425 years ago, Galileo Galilei, sometimes called the father of physics, laid a primitive scientific foundation for understanding the dynamics of the universe. Building on Galileo's work, a generation later, Sir Isaac Newton wrote that the observable universe had three dimensions.

Approximately 100 years ago, Albert Einstein suggested the universe has four dimensions, adding time as a component (or dimension) to solve his theory of relativity. Einstein's work, though helpful in understanding the largest of dynamics such as the retrograde measurement of planetary movement, and how we may project light shift due the gravitational impact of stars (or black holes), was not very useful in measuring things that were infinitesimally small. This gap gave rise to the development of *quantum physics*.

Since before the birth of Christ, secular philosophers have suggested the observable universe is not the only universe which exists. . However, the intensive study of quantum physics during the 20th century moved the idea of a multiverse from interesting musings to a widely held and accepted scientific view.

Many leading physicists today hold that the universe has multiple dimensions. Another way of stating this is that the multiverse is comprised of multiple planes of reality. In other words, as Star Trek aficionados would say – *it contains many parallel or alternate universes.*

Substantiating the multiverse theory was the early 20th century "double slit experiment." The experiment, first postulated in 1801 by the forward-thinking Thomas Young of England, found that light and matter particles can "change their nature."

The Scientific American Publication[96] profiled the findings of the experiment:

*"It clearly demonstrates the fundamental strangeness of quantum mechanics: that light, and matter as well, **is in fact both a particle and a wave**—a concept known as wave-particle duality. It also establishes the superposition principle: **particles can exist in multiple states and even simultaneously in multiple places.**"*

The experiment proved that something (in this case, a photon) could exist in two locations or occupy two different spaces simultaneously. In recent decades, this idea has been developed into what is known as String, Wave, M, and F theories. Each theory seeks a unifying formula to measure the big and the small and determine the number of dimensions in reality.

The M theory suggests there are 10 or 11 dimensions, while the F theory suggests 11 or 12. Some physicists suggest the number could be infinite.

In multiverse theory, life can exist in each plane or dimension. Theoretically, like the photon in the famed "double slit" experiment, all matter (or beings) can simultaneously exist on multiple planes and exhibit different natures and realities. This has been imagined in multiple science-fiction movies and television programs, perhaps, most notably, Star Trek. The original Star Trek television shows back in the 1960's featured ten alternate reality/parallel universe episodes.

However, pre-dating Star Trek writers, and even quantum physicists, Einstein, Newton, and Galileo, are a host of Old Testament writers who, inspired by the Holy Spirit, noted that God is omnipotent, omniscient, omnipresent, and the Creator of all. Simply put, Old Testament writers pointed to a multiverse, with God transcending and operating outside of our dimension and time.

Just as, at a rudimentary level, the famous "double slit" experiment showed that a photon can take on dual natures and be in multiple locations simultaneously, the Bible reveals that God also manifests Himself as having more than one Nature (the Father, Son, and Holy Spirit), and can exist in multiple locations at the same time. A few examples follow:

• The "one God" (Deut. 6:4) of Christianity is referenced by plural terms in Scripture. Plural terms include ***Elohim*** (Gen,1:1, 35:7; Deut. 4:28, 5:11, 7:18; Judges 11:24, 1 Kings 11:33, etc.), ***maker*** (Isaiah 54:5). and ***us*** (Gen. 1:26; Isa. 6:8).

• Jesus is presented as simultaneously being God and *sharing* in the work of God. A few verses that illustrate this follow.

o In the beginning was the word. The word was ***with God*** and the word ***was God."*** (John 1:1 – *emphasis added*).

o For ***by him*** were ***all things*** created, that are in heaven, and that are in earth, visible and invisible, whether they be thrones, or dominions, or principalities, or powers: ***all things were created by him***, and for him." (Col. 1:16 – *emphasis added*).

• In Scripture, Jesus is presented as being one with God (John 14:9) and yet had conversations with God (John 17).

• Scripture notes that Jesus allowed Himself to be crucified (John 10:18), that He laid His life down, and though dead raised it up again (John 10:17-18).

Additional thoughts:

● **God existed outside of and before our dimension/ universe existed:** Genesis indicates that God existed *before* creation. Genesis 1:1 begins: *"In the beginning, God created..."*

That thought is echoed in the New Testament where God, as Christ, is presented as creating "all things...that are in heaven..."[97] The "heaven" noted here is *our universe*. God existed before and outside of our reality. Paul repeats this truth later in the same verse, writing, "All things were created by him, and for him."

Though virtually impossible to fully comprehend, Scripture reveals that God *created* our universe—He did not fashion all there is out of what was—He created *what was*. He is the creator of all that is and all that will ever be. God's existence transcends what we know, can understand, or observe. He existed before our dimension/ universe/reality, created our dimension/universe/reality, and continuously engages with our dimension/universe/ reality. Using the language of contemporary science, God exists in another dimension—thus proving there is more than one dimension/plane/reality/universe.

● **Heaven is a reference to another dimension:** The Bible presents heaven as a different plane of existence... Elements are unfamiliar (Rev. 21:9-11) and beauty is amplified (Psalm 50:2). Scripture notes we cannot even imagine what we will see in heaven as it will be different from anything we have seen on earth (1 Cor. 2:9-11).

There will be life but not death (Rev. 21:4). There will be no hunger in heaven (Rev. 7:16) but there will be food

(Mark 14:25; Rev. 22:2). Unusual life forms are found in heaven, including the Seraphim, Cherubim, and the Four Living Creatures. There are relationships in heaven but no marriage (Matt. 22:30). In heaven there will be no tears (Rev. 21:4) and no darkness (Rev. 22:5).

Scripture speaks of heaven as a place (not a concept) and even presents measurements to some aspects of the Kingdom (see Revelation 21). However, most scholars believe those measurements are highly symbolic, representing perfection and purity, which are uncountable, infinite, or beyond imagination.

● **The nature of Jesus is beyond human:** Jesus' nature is not bound by the laws of this universe. He is perfect and eternal. The elements obeyed His commands—with a word He healed all manner of maladies. Scripture presents Jesus as master over life and death. The Lord's titles, miracles, foreknowledge, insight into what others were thinking, and well-documented ministry, indicate that Jesus lived on earth approximately 2000 years ago, but was not of this world.

● **Pillar of Fire:** In the story of Moses and the chosen people passing through the Red Sea,[98] God is revealed as leading the group away from Pharaoh's army, but the Divine 'pillar of fire' (the Holy Spirit), is different and separated from God. Similarly, in Ezekiel's vision of God[99] in Ezekiel 1, there are distinct separations of some aspects of the Divine. Note Ezekiel's depiction as recorded in the King James text:

4And I looked, and, behold, a whirlwind came out of the north, a great cloud, and a fire infolding itself, and a brightness was about it, and out of the midst thereof as the colour of amber, out of the midst of the fire.

*5Also out of the midst thereof came the likeness of four **living creatures**. [emphasis added] And this was their appearance; they had the likeness of a man.*

6And every one had four faces, and every one had four wings.

7And their feet were straight feet; and the sole of their feet was like the sole of a calf's foot: and they sparkled like the colour of burnished brass.

8And they had the hands of a man under their wings on their four sides, and they four had their faces and their wings.

9Their wings were joined one to another; they turned not when they went; they went every one straight forward.

10As for the likeness of their faces, they four had the face of a man, and the face of a lion, on the right side: and they four had the face of an ox on the left side; they four also had the face of an eagle.

11Thus were their faces: and their wings were stretched upward; two wings of every one were joined one to another, and two covered their bodies.

12And they went every one straight forward: whither the spirit was to go, they went; and they turned not when they went.

13As for the likeness of the living creatures, their appearance was like burning coals of fire, and like the appearance of lamps: it went up and down among the living creatures; and the fire was bright, and out of the fire went forth lightning.

14And the living creatures ran and returned as the appearance of a flash of lightning.

*15Now as I beheld the living creatures, **behold one wheel upon the earth by the living creatures,** [emphasis added] with his four faces.*

*16The appearance of the wheels and their work was like unto the colour of a beryl: and they four had one likeness: and their appearance and their work was as it were a **wheel in the middle of a wheel.*** [emphasis added]

17When they went, they went upon their four sides: and they turned not when they went.

18As for their rings, they were so high that they were dreadful; and their rings were full of eyes round about them four.

*19And **when the living creatures went, the wheels went by them**:* [emphasis added] *and when the living creatures were lifted up from the earth, the wheels were lifted up.*

*20Whithersoever the spirit was to go, they went, thither was their spirit to go; and the wheels were lifted up over against them: **for the spirit of the living creature was in the wheels** [emphasis added].*

*21When those went, these went; and when those stood, these stood; and when those were lifted up from the earth, the wheels were lifted up over against them: **for the spirit of the living creature was in the wheels** [emphasis added].*

22And the likeness of the firmament upon the heads of the living creature was as the colour of the terrible crystal, stretched forth over their heads above.

23And under the firmament were their wings straight, the one toward the other: every one had two, which covered on this side, and every one had two, which covered on that side, their bodies.

24And when they went, I heard the noise of their wings, like the noise of great waters, as the voice of the Almighty, the voice of speech, as the noise of an host: when they stood, they let down their wings.

^{25}*And there was a voice from the firmament that was over their heads, when they stood, and had let down their wings.*

^{26}*And above the firmament that was over their heads was the likeness of a throne, as the appearance of a sapphire stone: and upon the likeness of the throne was the likeness as the appearance of a man above upon it.*

^{27}*And I saw as the colour of amber, as the appearance of fire round about within it, from the appearance of his loins even upward, and from the appearance of his loins even downward, I saw as it were the appearance of fire, and it had brightness round about.*

^{28}*As the appearance of the bow that is in the cloud in the day of rain, so was the appearance of the brightness round about. This was the appearance of the likeness of the glory of the Lord. And when I saw it, I fell upon my face, and I heard a voice of one that spake.*

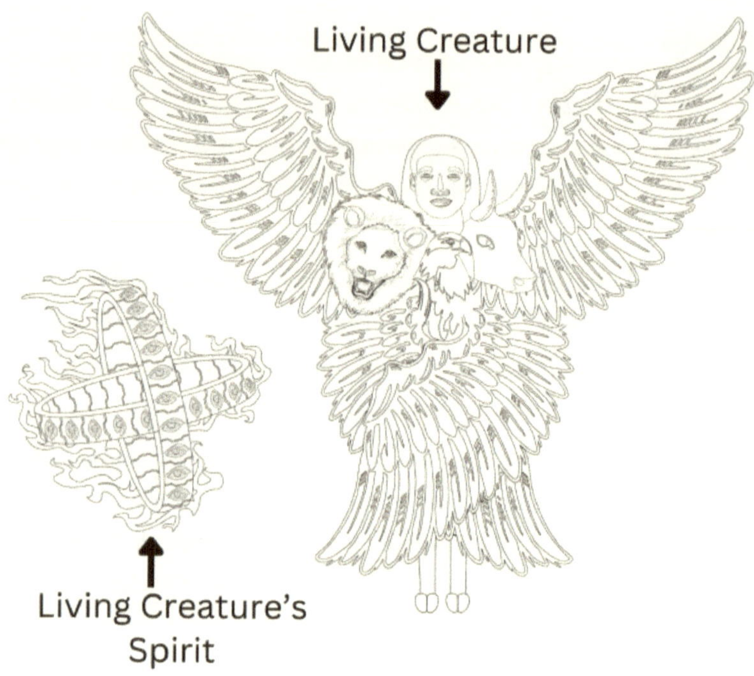

In Ezekiel chapter 1, the prophet describes a vision he receives from God. In this vision, a living thing—often called a cherub or a living creature—is present, along with its own spirit. The description of this living being and its spirit suggests that they are not attached to one another in the traditional three-dimensional sense but rather exist separately yet are still one.

The vision described in Ezekiel Chapter 1 is filled with vivid imagery and symbolism. The living being is described as having the appearance of a man but with four faces—those of a lion, an ox, an eagle, and a human. It also has four wings and stands next to wheels covered in eyes. This description highlights the otherworldly nature of the being, emphasizing that it is not simply a human but something more.

Ezekiel also describes the spirit. This spirit is described as being the living creature's very own spirit but also separate from it. The spirit is described as moving the wheels on which the living being stood next too. This separation between the living being and its spirit suggests that they are distinct entities yet still connected in some way.

This concept of the living being and its spirit being separate (but one) can be compared to the idea of a Triune God. This concept can be difficult to understand and explain, but it highlights the mystery and complexity of God's Nature. This suggests that there is a deeper level of unity and oneness that goes beyond our understanding. Just as the Triune God is One in essence but exists in three Persons, the living being and its spirit in Ezekiel's vision are separate yet united in some way that surpasses our human comprehension.

The Triune Nature of God is indeed a mystery—it transcends our reality, perceptions, and imagination. Yet, biblical writers affirm the dual nature of Christ (human and Divine), the Triune Nature of God, and that God's domain operates outside of our time and laws of physics—i.e., *within another dimension.*

Science acknowledges the probability of a multiverse—science should, in turn, acknowledge the probability of a God who created the multiverse and manifests Himself in a Triune fashion as He interfaces between **our** physical and **His** spiritual plane.

Chapter 11: Monotheism and the Plurality of God in Jewish Literature

Multiverse—science should, in turn, acknowledge the probability of a God Who created the multiverse and manifests in various forms throughout it. The existence of a Higher Power that designs and oversees the multiverse could explain its intricate complexity and order. This acknowledgement would bridge the gap between science and religion and offer a deeper understanding of the universe and our place within it.

Judaism recognizes that certain Divine instructions (such as atoning for sins via animal sacrifices) were given by God with a specific application in mind. That is, God's specific spiritual instructions for those living before the Flood were different from the Lord's expectations for Hebrews living during the time of Moses, and those expectations differed for Hebrews living in Babylon or Persia during the period known as the Babylonian exile. However, while understanding that the application of some biblical directives varies over time—having a particular binding force in particular periods of history—understanding God's Nature is an amazing constant.

From the Jewish point of view, the understanding of God's Nature has not substantially changed since the dawn of humanity—God is "One," yet more than One.

The terms to describe God in Genesis 1 (Elohim) and Genesis 3 (us) are plural. These terms originate from sacred oral accounts of the creation story, passed down from Adam to Enoch to Noah to Abraham, and ultimately to Moses, whom God inspired to put the account into writing.

Moses' writings present God as the one true God. He wrote in Deuteronomy 6:4, *"Hear, O Israel: The Lord our God is one Lord."*

This verse became one of the keystone verses of the Old Testament, just as John 3:16 is a keystone New Testament verse.

Referred to as the *Shema* ("to hear"), Deuteronomy 6:4 is followed by instructions in verse 7 and again in 11:18-19. In these follow-up verses, Hebrews were commanded to "speak...these words...when you lie down and when you get up." According to Jewish scholar Dr. Jeffrey Tigay, by the late Second Temple period, the directive became incorporated into Jewish law (the halakhic), with the expectation being that all Hebews would recite this verse and offer prayers in the morning (the *Keri'at Shema)* and at the end of the day.[100]

However, though the Hebrews affirmed that God is One, it is evident that Hebrews also believed the one God manifests a multi-dimensional nature. This is alluded to in Genesis 1 where God and the Holy Spirit share in the work of creation; in Genesis 3 where God counsels with Himself after humans eat of the forbidden fruit; and in Exodus when the wondrous power of the Holy Spirit is presented as working with God, separate from God, yet one with God. The Triune Nature of God is also foreshadowed in Genesis 18 when three heavenly beings visit Abraham and later, in Isaiah 54:5 when the plural word *maker* is used to reference God.

The multidimensional Nature of God—the belief that God is One and yet, more than One—is a foundational, immutable facet of Jewish theology. It predates the writings of Moses, is incorporated into the writings of Moses, and is echoed in the writings of the Psalms and prophets.

An article titled *Early Jewish Conceptions of God* noted that Second Temple period Jewish writings also include a body of literature called the *heikhalot.* The writings are mystical in nature and are often at variance with what Christians today refer to as the Old Testament text. These writings are said to originate from visions and detail how God has a kind of physical (or measurable) presence (for example, "a neck 130.8 million miles in length and fingers each 150.3 million miles long") but is also spirit and omnipresent.[101]

Philo of Alexandria (20 BC-50 AD) is among the late second-period Jewish writers who contemplated the Nature of God. In many ways, his writings mirror those of the *tannaim*[1] (early contributors to the *Mishnah*). In his writing, Philo integrated Greek philosophy with Jewish tradition and presented the Nature of God in an abstract philosophical way.

Philo wrote of God as having two great powers, known as *God and the Logos*.[102] He expounds on the multidimensional Nature of God by writing of the three who visited Abraham in Genesis 18:

> "He did not [at first] perceive that they were in reality of a more divine nature... but took every possible pains to make their extemporaneous reception worthy of them... and he said to his wife, 'Hasten now, and make ready quickly three measures of fine meal,' and he himself went forth among the herds of oxen, and brought forth a tender and well-fed heifer, and gave it to his servant...[The three] had changed their spiritual and soul-like essence, and assumed the appearance of men...And by being wholly surrounded with...brilliancy...free from all shade or darkness, [Abraham] then perceived a threefold image of one subject, one image of the living God, and others of the other two..."[103]

Dr. Doure wrote of Philo: "The philosophical doctrine of the powers... allowed Philo to maintain both the oneness of God despite His many names...and the transcendence of God despite His action on the world."[104]

---

1. *https://www.myjewishlearning.com/texts/Rabbinics/Talmud/Talmud/Studying_Talmud/ Tannaim_and_Amoraim.shtml*

The book *Novatian: The Trinity, The Spectacles, Jewish Foods, In Praise of Purity, Letters of the Shepherds*,[105] presents a scholarly review of late Second Temple religious thoughts and notes that Jews of this period argued against the Triune Nature of God by primarily leaning on four rather esoteric arguments:

1. "[There is] no distinction between the Son of God and the Son of Man. For if a distinction were made, it would not be difficult to prove that Jesus Christ is both Man and God."

2. "They would have it appear that one and the self-same man—that is, the Son of Man—is also the Son of God, so that the man and the flesh and that self-same frail bodily substance is said to be the Son of God. Therefore, since no distinction is made between the Son of Man and the Son of God and since they claim that the Son of Man Himself is the Son of God, they assert that Christ, as a mere man, is likewise the Son of God.

3. "The pre-eminence of that name, "Son of God," resides in the Spirit of the Lord who descended and came; whereas the sequela of that name is to be found in the Son of God and Man. In consequence [of such a union] this Son of Man rightly became the Son of God, although He is not primarily the Son of God."

4. "Accordingly, the angel, aware of that arrangement and making known the providential order of the mystery, did not confuse everything so as not to leave any vestige of a distinction. He made that distinction when he announced: "Therefore also that holy thing to be born of thee shall be called the Son of God." For if he had not

allotted that partition [of natures] with its due balance but had left it in hazy confusion, he would have undoubtedly given the heretics an opportunity to declare that the Son of Man, as man, is the same Son both of God and Man."

Regarding how first-century AD Jews viewed the nature or Deity of Christ, Dr.'s Hastings, Selbie, and Lambert in *Christ in Jewish Literature* write that "the relations between Jews and Christians during that period have usually been far from friendly...[and] references to Christ in the writings of Jews are, comparatively speaking, few and unimportant." [106]

The scholars add that Jewish leaders of that era often chose to ignore Jesus's ministry, noting that "references to Christ are a mere drop in the ocean of the Talmud." However, by the medieval period, Rabbinic literature condemning Jesus as a heretic was rampant, with a large collection of such writings comprising a work called the *Tŏl'dŏth Jĕshū.*

Talmudic literature refers to Jesus as *ha-Nŏtzri,* B. Stada, or B. Pandira.[107] Talmudic contributions note that...

- Jesus was born out of wedlock (M. *Jeb.* iv. 13, cf. Bab. *Shabb.* 104*b*).

- Jesus' mother was called Miriam, a dresser of women's hair (Bab. *Shab. Ib*).

- Miriam's husband was Pappus b. Judah and her paramour was Pandira.

- Miriam claimed to be a descendant of princes and rulers, but was not.

● Miriam "played the harlot with a carpenter" (Bab. *Sanh.* 106*a*).

● Jesus had spent time in Egypt and learned "magic" there.

● Jesus was a worker of dark arts and deceived many.

● Jesus sinned and caused the multitude to sin (Bab. *Sanh.* 107*b*).

● Jesus "mocked at the words of the wise, and was excommunicated" (*ib.*).

● Jesus was "tainted with heresy (*ib.* 103*a*).

● Jesus "called himself God, also the Son of Man, and said that he would go up to heaven (Jerus. *Taan.* 65*b*).

● Jesus resurrected ("made himself live") by the name of God (Bab. *Sanh.* 106*a*).

● Jesus was "tried in Lydda (a city approximately 25 miles north of Jerusalem) as a deceiver and as a teacher of apostasy" (Tos. *Sanh.* x. 11; Jerus. *Sanh.* 25*c, d*).

● Jesus "was executed in Lydda, on the eve of Passover, which was also the eve of Sabbath" (*ib.* and Tos. *Sanh.* ix. 7).

● Jesus ("under the curse and name of Balaam") "was put to death by Pinḥas the Robber (Pontius Pilatus), and at the time was thirty-three years old" (Bab. *Sanh.* 106*b*).

There are a few references to Jesus in the Mischna, which is a collection of wisdom literature and commentary on the Law completed in about 220 AD. The Mischna affirms the traditional Hebrew view of God, and acknowledges Jesus as a healer from Nazareth, but repudiates his claims to Deity and indicates he used sorcery to deceive the people. Mischna writings also affirm the crucifixion, and Jesus is referenced as Jēshū ha-Nōtzri (*i.e.* the Nazarene). Jesus is also referred to as...[108]

- "One who practiced magic, and deceived and led astray Israel" (Bab. *Sanh.* 107*b*).

- "Having five disciples" (Bab. *Sanh.* 43*a*, 'Jēshū (ha-Nōtzri).

- "There came in Jacob, a man of Chephar Sechanja, to cure...in the name of Jēshū" (Tos. *Ḥ*. 22, 23).

- "On the eve of Passover they hung Jēshū ha-Nōtzri" (Bab. *Sanh.* 43*a*).

Rabbinical writing about Jesus started with Rabbi Eliezer b. Horkenos. Eliezer was a disciple of Rabbi Joḥanan b. Zaccai, who lived in Jerusalem when Jesus was crucified. His brother-in-law was Rabbi Gamaliel—he was the grandson of the Gamaliel referenced in the book of Acts. His writings, along with the writings of Rabbi Judah the Holy, and Rabbis Akiba and Meir, affirm Jesus' existence, and some aspects of the Gospel narrative (such as his miracles, trial, and crucifixion). However, these first and second-century AD Rabbinic writings reject the notion that Jesus was an expression of the One (but multidimensional) God of the Old Testament.[109]

Josephus's *Against Apion 2,*[110] indicate that the Hellenized Jews of this period often understood Jesus' teaching to be allegorical or as general "summaries of God's Law." Casting Jesus as a philosopher or mystic disallowed his claims to Deity and to any references that He was in unity with the wisdom and transcendence of God and God's plan to bring Divine justice on Earth.[111]

Another collection of commentary and wisdom literature, the *Tosefta*, began to be compiled less than 50 years after the completion of the Mischna. *Tosefta* is an Aramaic term meaning "additions" and is often written in the plural form, *Tosafot*. This commentary on the Mishnah was written by Rabbis between the second and fourth centuries ad.[112]

Writings in the *Tosefta* make no changes to the long-standing Hebrew view of God, His Oneness, and His multidimensional Nature. The writings do not mention Jesus, but affirm the views of Jewish religious leaders who, they posit, represent a Divinely appointed line of succession going back to Moses. We read: "Moses received Torah from Sinai and handed it on to Joshua and ending with the names of authorities of the first and second centuries. Some of these, in particular Gamaliel and his son Simeon, are known to us as Pharisees."[113]

The *Midrash*, a collection of Jewish religious literature primarily written between 250-500 AD, affirms that the "Spirit of the Lord that is spoken of in Isaiah...is the same Spirit of the Lord that moved over the primeval waters of Creation."[114] This view reflects perfect unity with the views of Old Testament-era Jews regarding the Nature of God.

A passage in First Enoch (62:5–9), written in the Second Temple Era, put in writing what many Jews slowly came to believe, that Jesus, the Son of Man, is also the Son of God—Emmanuel—the One God who came to live among us. The unknown Jewish author of First Enoch wrote:

"And the kings and the mighty and all who possess the land

will bless and glorify and exalt him who rules over all, who was hidden.

For from the beginning, the Son of Man was hidden,

and the Most High preserved him in the presence of his might,

and he revealed him to the chosen...

"And all the kings and the mighty and the exalted and those who rule the land will fall on their faces in his presence;

"and they will worship and set their hope on the Son of Man,

and they will supplicate and petition for mercy from him."

Maimonides, the great 12th-century Jewish scholar and philosopher, affirmed the Hebrew's iron-clad view of the Oneness of God, writing, "To believe in the oneness of God is a positive commandment and anyone who thinks there is another god has violated the great principle upon which everything depends."[115] However, one falls short when one believes that God can do all things, but cannot be Triune in Nature.

Though sometimes veiled in Scripture, the thought that God would redeem humanity and that the Messiah, the Redeemer, is the very expression of God—*God in the flesh*—flows from the early pages of Genesis. Sadly, for most Jews, a profound spiritual blindness has kept them from seeing that Jesus is the fulfillment of the Law, and the last and final Person in the Trinity.

Himself in a Triune fashion as He interfaces between our physical and His spiritual plane.

Glossary

Adonai: A Hebrew word used in the Old Testament to refer to God as the Lord and Master, signifying His authority and sovereignty over all.

Adumbrated: means to foreshadow vaguely, to give a vague outline, to obscure or overshadow or sketch something in a brief or symbolic way.

Cherry-picking: In biblical theology, this refers to the selective or biased interpretation of scripture, choosing specific verses or passages to support a particular belief or agenda while disregarding the broader context or full teachings of the Bible.

Christophany: Refers to an appearance or manifestation of Christ in the Old Testament before His incarnation as Jesus Christ.

Co-equality: Refers to the concept within the Christian doctrine of the Trinity, which states that the Father, the Son (Jesus Christ), and the Holy Spirit are equally and fully God. This means that each Person of the Trinity possesses the exact Divine Nature, attributes, and authority.

Economic Trinity: Refers to the scripturally supported understanding of the distinct roles and functions of the Father, Son, and Holy Spirit in relation to the created order and the plan of salvation. This concept acknowledges their cooperative work in the economy of redemption while affirming their complete equality in nature and essence within the Trinity.

Elohim: Is a Hebrew word that is often used in the Bible to refer to God, especially in the Old Testament. It is a plural form of the word "Eloah," meaning "god" or "gods."

Emmanuel or Immanuel: Translates to "God is with us" and is often used to refer to the presence of God among humanity, particularly in Christian theology.

Hermeneutics: Is the study of interpreting and understanding written texts, particularly within the context of biblical studies. It involves methods and principles for analyzing and comprehending the meaning and significance of sacred writings.

Hypostatic Union: Is the belief that Jesus is fully God and fully man, without the two natures being mixed, divided, or changed.

Law of Dharma: rooted in Hindu and Buddhist teachings, refers to the moral and ethical duty that governs an individual's life. It encompasses the idea of living in accordance with one's spiritual and moral obligations, fulfilling one's responsibilities, and striving for righteousness and virtue in all actions.

Lord: In the Bible, "Lord" can refer to God as the Divine ruler and master, and in the New Testament, it is used to address Jesus Christ as the Messiah and Divine Son of God.

LORD: In many English translations of the Bible, "LORD" in all capital letters represents the Divine name YHWH (Yahweh) in the Old Testament, signifying the personal and covenantal relationship between God and His people.

Modalism: Is a belief that teaches that the Father, Son, and Holy Spirit are not distinct Persons within the Godhead but rather different modes or manifestations of the same God.

Ontological: Refers to the branch of metaphysics dealing with the nature of being. In a biblical context, it could be used to discuss the nature of God, Jesus, the Holy Spirit, or the study of God's existence and essential nature.

Original Sin: A doctrine that asserts that all people have a sinful nature as a result of Adam and Eve's disobedience in the Garden of Eden, as described in the book of Genesis. This doctrine suggests that all humans are born with a tendency to sin and need redemption through the grace of God.

Patristic: Refers to the early Christian theologians known as the Church Fathers, who lived and wrote during the first centuries of Christianity.

Polytheist or Pantheon: Is someone who believes in the existence of multiple gods or deities.

Progressive Revelation: refers to the concept in theology that Divine knowledge and understanding are revealed gradually over time, leading to a deeper comprehension of spiritual truths.

Salvific: Refers to having the quality of bringing about salvation or being related to the act of saving or delivering from sin or its consequences.

Subordinationism: Refers to the erroneous belief that suggests a form of subordination or inequality within the Trinity, particularly in relation to the roles and essence of the Father, Son, and Holy Spirit. This concept has been historically regarded as heretical within Christian theology due to its implications of hierarchy and inequality among the Divine Persons.

Tetragrammaton: Refers to the four Hebrew letters YHVH or YHWH, which represent the sacred name of God in the Hebrew Bible. It is often transliterated as Yahweh or Jehovah.

Theistic: Refers to the belief in the existence of one or more gods or deities who are involved in the creation, maintenance, and governance of the universe.

Trans-theistic: Refers to spiritual or religious perspectives that transcend the traditional theistic concept of God as a personal deity or deities. Instead of focusing on the worship of gods, trans-theistic beliefs might emphasize universal principles, enlightenment, the nature of existence, or the pursuit of spiritual understanding beyond the confines of theistic frameworks.

Tritheism: Is the belief in three separate gods within the context of the Christian doctrine of the Trinity, as opposed to the traditional understanding of one God in three Persons.

Unitarians: These are individuals or groups that adhere to Unitarianism, a theological belief that rejects the doctrine of the Trinity and emphasizes God's oneness and Jesus Christ's humanity rather than his Divinity.

Table of Authorities

Alexander, T. Desmond, and David Weston Baker. *Dictionary of the Old Testament: Pentateuch*. IVP, 2003.

Aristides, *Apology*, Greek version.

Arndt, William et al. *A Greek-English Lexicon of the New Testament and Other Early Christian Literature*. Chicago, University of Chicago Press, 2000.

Beard, David A. *The Errors of the Trinity*. Bloomington, IN, Author House, 2003.

Bell, Rob. *Velvet Elvis*. Grand Rapids, Zondervan, 2005.

Brown, Dan. *The Da Vinci Code*. New York, Anchor Books, 2006.

Clement of Alexandria, *Exhortation to the Heathen*, 1, Ante-Nicene Fathers (hereafter abbreviated ANF).

Clement. *First Epistle to the Corinthians*, Translation from Michael Holmes, vol. 43, The Apostolic Fathers, Grand Rapids, Baker Academic, 2007.

Clement of Alexandria, et al. *"Fragments of Clemens Alexandrinus," in Fathers of the Second Century*. Edited by Alexander Roberts, et al., translated by William Wilson, vol. 2, The Ante-Nicene Fathers, Buffalo, Christian Literature Company, 1885.

Duke, Charles. "The Works of Philo by C. D. Yonge." *Early Christian Writings,* https://www.earlychristianwritings.com/yonge/index.html. Accessed 7 April 2024.

"Early Jewish Conceptions of God." *My Jewish Learning*, https://www.myjewishlearning.com/article/early-jewish-conceptions-of-god/. Accessed 11 March 2024.

Editors at Inspired Philosophy. "The Trinity Explained." 4 November 2016, https://www.youtube.com/watch?v=0G2S5ziDcO0.[1] Accessed 12 February 2024.

Filler, Elad, Translated by Michael Carasik, Philo's Threefold Divine Vision and the Christian Trinity. *Hebrew Union College Annual*, *87*, *93–113*. https://doi.org/10.15650/hebruniocollannu.87.2016.0093, 2016, Accessed 2 February 2024.

Genesis Rabbah 1:2, 6th Century. I, Dr. Jeffrey Johnson, *God Was There, Genesis Chapters 1-12*, Eugene, OR, Wipf and Stock Publishers, 2005

Halton, Thomas P., editor. *Leo the Great Sermons*. Translated by Jane Patricia Freeland and Agnes Josephine Conway, vol. 93, *The Fathers of the Church*, Washington, DC, The Catholic University of America Press, 1996.

Hastings, John, et al. editors, "Christ," *A Dictionary of Christ and the Gospels: Aaron–Zion*, Edinburgh; New York: T&T Clark; Charles Scribner's Sons, 1906.

Hippolytus, *Refutation of All Heresies*, 10.29. ANF.

---

1. https://www.youtube.com/watch?v=0G2S5ziDcO0

Horst, Pieter W. van der, "Jewish Literature: Historians and Poets," *Dictionary of New Testament Background: A Compendium of Contemporary Biblical Scholarship*, Downers Grove, IL: InterVarsity Press, 2000.

Ignatius, *Letter to the Ephesians*, 18.2. Holmes, ANF.
Ignatius, *Letter to Polycarp*, 3.2. Holmes, ANF.
Ignatius, *Letter to the Smyrnaeans*, 1.1. Holmes, ANF.

Irenaeus, *Against Heresies*, 2.1.1. ANF.
Josephus's *Against Apion*, 2.

Kelley II, M. J. *Divine Revelation: Unveiling Jesus as God.* Self-published, 2023.

Lackey, P. R. *The Tyranny of the Trinity.* Bloomington, Author House, 2001.

Lewis, C. S. *Mere Christianity.* Geoffrey Bles, 1952.

Martyr, Justin, *First Apology*, 63. ANF, I:184. / Martyr, *Dialogue with Trypho*, 126. ANF.
McDowell, Josh. *Evidence That Demands A Verdict*, Nashville, Thomas Nelson, 2017 Edition.
Melito, 5. ANF.
Mishneh Torah, *Yesodey ha-Torah.*

Neusner, Jacob, "Rabbinic Literature: Mishnah and Tosefta," *Dictionary of New Testament Background: A Compendium of Contemporary Biblical Scholarship*, Downers Grove, IL: InterVarsity Press, 2000.

Novatian, *The Trinity, The Spectacles, Jewish Foods, In Praise of Purity, Letters*, ed. Hermigild Dressler, trans.

Russell J. DeSimone, vol. 67, The Fathers of the Church, Washington, DC: The Catholic University of America Press, 1974.

Novatian, *On the Trinity,* 11. ANF, V:620. Cf. Novatian, Treatise Concerning the Trinity.
Origen, *De Principiis,* Preface, 4. ANF.

Page, T. E., and W.H. D. Rouse, editors. *Augustine of Hippo, St. Augustine's Confessions.* Translated by William Watts, vol. 2, New York, The Loeb Classical Library, 1912.

Patzia, Arthur G., and Petrotta, Anthony J., *Pocket Dictionary of Biblical Studies,* Downers Grove, IL: InterVarsity Press, 2002.

Polycarp, *Philippians 12:2.* Holmes, AF.
Runia, David, *Philo of Alexandria: An Annotated Bibliography,* Radice and Runia, 2000.

Sinha, Urbasi. "Quantum Slits Open New Doors." *Scientific American,* 1 January 2020, https://www.scientificamerican.com/article/quantum-slits-open-new-doors/. Accessed 11 March 2024.

Smith, J. Z., *Dying and rising Gods.* In L. Jones (Ed.), Encyclopedia of religion (2nd ed., Vol. 5, pp. 2535–2540). New York: Macmillan, 2005.

Spears, Robert. *The Unitarian Handbook of Scriptural Illustrations & Expositions.* London, British and Foreign Unitarian Association, 1883.

Spurgeon, CH. "Bible Text Commentaries by Don Stewart." *Blue Letter Bible,* https://www.blueletterbible.org/commentaries/ stewart_don/ Accessed 30 February 2024.

Tatian, *Address to the Greeks,* 21. ANF.
Tertullian, *Against Hermogenes,* 17. ANF.
Tertullian, *Against Praxeas,* 25. ANF.
Tertullian, *Apology,* 21. ANF.
Tertullian, *Treatise on the Soul,* 41. ANF.
Theophilus, *Epistle to Autolycus,* 3.23. ANF, II.

Tigay, Jeffrey H. *Deuteronomy, The JPS Torah Commentary.* Jewish Publication Society, 1996.

Tigay, Jeffrey. "*Deuteronomy 6:4—The Shema.*" My Jewish Learning, https://www.myjewishlearning.com/article/ deuteronomy-64-the-shema/. Accessed 11 April 2024.

Upton, John. "Ancient Sea Rise Tale Told Accurately for 10000 Years." *Scientific American,* 26 January 2015, https://www.scientificamerican.com/article/ancient-sea-rise-tale-told-accurately-for-10-000-years/. Accessed 11 March 2024.

Wallace, Daniel B. *Greek Grammar beyond the Basics: An Exegetical Syntax of the New Testament.* New York, Harper Collins, 1996.

Warfield, B. B. *The International Bible Encyclopaedia.* Edited by James Orr, Grand Rapids, Eerdmans, 1930.

Whiston, Josephus and William. *The Works of Josephus: Complete and Unabridged.* Peabody: Hendrickson, 1987.

Wikipedia, Is there scientific evidence that oral tradition can preserve historical facts for a long time, centuries or even milleniums, in an intact state? : r/AskHistorians[2]. Accessed 11 March 2024.

---

2. https://www.reddit.com/r/AskHistorians/comments/9dtmk0/
   is_there_scientific_evidence_that_oral_tradition/

Page

[1] B. B. Warfield, *The International Bible Encyclopaedia*, James Orr, ed. (Grand Rapids: Eerdmans, 1930), 3012.

[2] C.S. Lewis, *Mere Christianity,* 162 (1952; Geoffrey Bles)

[3] Matthew 4:1-11

[4] Proverbs 25:2

[5] Romans 6:23

[6] Hebrews 11:6

[7] John 10:30

[8] Acts 7:30-35

[9] Acts 1:8

[10] Psalm 91:11-12

[11] Genesis 1:3

[12] Genesis 14:18

[13] Deuteronomy 33:17

[14] Genesis 1:1

[15] M.J. Kelley II, *Divine Revelation: Unveiling Jesus as God* (self-published, 2023) 63

[16] Psalm 19:1-6

[17] Matthew 7:23

[18] Alexander, T. Desmond, and David Weston Baker. 2003. *Dictionary of the Old Testament: Pentateuch.* IVP.

[19]   Tigay, Jeffrey H. *Deuteronomy, The JPS Torah Commentary* (Philadelphia: Jewish Publication Society, 1996), 76.

[20] Exodus 20:3

[21] Matthew 22:36-40

[22] Genesis 1:26-27

[23] Josephus and William Whiston, *The Works of Josephus: Complete and Unabridged* (Peabody: Hendrickson, 1987), 29.

[24] Ezekiel 1:10

[25] Isaiah 6:2

[26] *Augustine of Hippo, St. Augustine's Confessions,* Vol. 2, ed. T. E. Page and W. H. D. Rouse, trans. William Watts, The Loeb Classical Library (New York; London: The Macmillan Co.; William Heinemann, 1912), 431–433

[27]   The Trinity Explained . (2016, November 4). [Video]. Retrieved February 12, 2024, from https://www.youtube.com/watch?v=0G2S5ziDcO0

[28] Jude 1:9

[29] Isaiah 42:8

[30] Isaiah 6:1-5

[31] Habakkuk 1:13

[32] Isaiah 41:10

[33] John 6:46-58

[34] John 1:18

[35] 1 Timothy 2:5

[36] Genesis 3

[37] 1 Corinthians 14:33

[38] Genesis 22:1; Matthew 27:46; Mark 15:34

[39] Psalm 12:6-7

[40] 2 Timothy 2:15

[41] Wallace, Daniel B. 1996. *Greek Grammar Beyond the Basics: An Exegetical Syntax of the New Testament*. Harper Collins.

[42] Ibid.

[43] Psalm 147:5

[44] John 1:1

[45] Clement of Alexandria, "Fragments of Clemens Alexandrinus," in Fathers of the Second Century: Hermas, Tatian, Athenagoras, Theophilus, and Clement of Alexandria (Entire), ed. Alexander Roberts, James Donaldson, and A. Cleveland Coxe, trans. William Wilson, vol. 2, The Ante-Nicene Fathers (Buffalo, NY: Christian Literature Company, 1885), 574.

[46] Leo the Great, Sermons, ed. Thomas P. Halton, trans. Jane Patricia Freeland and Agnes Josephine Conway, vol. 93, The Fathers of the Church (Washington, DC: The Catholic University of America Press, 1996), 92.

[47] William Arndt et al., *A Greek-English Lexicon of the New Testament and Other Early Christian Literature* (Chicago: University of Chicago Press, 2000), 33.

[48] David A. Beard, *The Errors of the Trinity* (Bloomington, IN: Author House, 2003), 28.

[49] Dan Brown, *The Da Vinci Code* (New York: Anchor Books, 2006), 253. This statement is made by one of Brown's literary characters, Sir Leigh Teabing.

[50] P. R. Lackey, *The Tyranny of the Trinity* (Bloomington, IN: Author House, 2001).

[51] Robert Spears, *The Unitarian Handbook of Scriptural Illustrations & Expositions* (London: British and Foreign Unitarian Association, 1883), 96.

[52] Rob Bell, *Velvet Elvis* (Grand Rapids: Zondervan, 2005), 22.

[53] https://www.blueletterbible.org/commentaries/stewart_don/

[54] John 8:58

[55] Matthew 1:23

[56] Isaiah 9:6

[57] John 14:9

[58] John 10:30

[59] ca.180 Theophilus, bishop of Antioch, writing to Autolycus (an apology for Christianity written around 180 AD), 99.

[60] Clement, *First Epistle to the Corinthians*, 43. Translation from Michael Holmes, The Apostolic Fathers (Grand Rapids: Baker Academic, 2007), 103 [Apostolic Fathers is hereafter AF].

[61] Aristides, *Apology*, Greek version, 15.

[62] Theophilus, *Epistle to Autolycus*, 3.23. ANF, II:118.

[63] Irenaeus, *Against Heresies*, 2.1.1. Ante-Nicene Fathers (hereafter abbreviated ANF), I:359.

[64] Ibid., 2.2.5. ANF, I:362.

[65] Ibid., 3.1.1–2. ANF, I:414–15.

[66] Tertullian, *Treatise on the Soul*, 41. ANF, III:221.

[67] Tertullian, *Apology*, 21. ANF, III:34–35.

[68] Tertullian, *Against Praxeas,* 25. ANF, III:608

[69] Tertullian, *Against Hermogenes*, 17. ANF, III:486–87.

[70] Ignatius, *Letter to the Ephesians*, 18.2. Holmes, AF, 197.

[71] Ibid., 19.3. Holmes, AF, 199.

[72] Ignatius, *Letter to the Smyrnaeans*, 1.1. Holmes, AF, 249.

[73] Ignatius, *Letter to Polycarp*, 3.2. Holmes, AF, 265.

[74] Polycarp, *Philippians 12:2*. Holmes, AF, 295.

[75] Martyr, Justin, *First Apology*, 63. ANF, I:184. / Martyr, *Dialogue with Trypho*, 126. ANF, I:263.

[76] Tatian, *Address to the Greeks*, 21. ANF, II:74.

[77] Melito, 5. ANF, VIII:757.

[78] Irenaeus, *Against Heresies*, 3.19.2. ANF, I:449.

[79] Ibid., 1.10.1. ANF, I:330.

[80] Ibid., 4.5.2. ANF, I:467.

[81] Ibid., 4.6.7. ANF, I:469.

[82] Clement of Alexandria, *Exhortation to the Heathen*, 1. ANF, II:173.

[83] Hippolytus, *Refutation of All Heresies*, 10.29. ANF, V:151.

[84] Origen, *De Principiis,* Preface, 4. ANF, IV:240.

[85] Novatian, *On the Trinity,* 11. ANF, V:620. Cf. Novatian, Treatise Concerning the Trinity, 15, 16, 26, 31.

[86] Genesis 11.

[87] Smith, J. Z. (2005). *Dying and rising Gods.* In L. Jones (Ed.), Encyclopedia of religion (2nd ed., Vol. 5, pp. 2535–2540). New York: Macmillan.

[88] McDowell, Josh. *Evidence That Demands A Verdict* (Thomas Nelson, Nashville. 2017 Edition) 205-230

[89] Matthew 5:17

[90] https://www.scientificamerican.com/article/ancient-sea-rise-tale-told-accurately-for-10-000-years/

[91] https://www.reddit.com/r/AskHistorians/comments/9dtmk0/is_there_scientific_evidence_that_oral_tradition/

[92] Justin Martyr, First Apology, 63. ANF, I:184. / Martyr, Dialogue with Trypho, 126. ANF, I:263.

[93] Irenaeus, Against Heresies, 2.1.1. ANF, I:359.

[94] Tertullian, Apology, 21. ANF, III:34–35.

[95] Tertullian, Against Praxeas, 25. ANF, III:608.

[96] Quantum Slits Open New Doors | Scientific American[3]

[97] Colossians 1:16

[98] Exodus 13

[99] Ezekiel 1:4-28

[100] Deuteronomy 6:4 – The Shema. *Article from My Jewish Learning Center* by Dr. Jeffrey Tigay, January, 2017. https://www.myjewishlearning.com/article/deuteronomy-64-the-shema/

[101] *Early Jewish Conceptions of God* https://www.myjewishlearning.com/article/early-jewish-conceptions-of-god/

[102] *The Works of Philo > Book 22.* https://www.earlychristianwritings.com/yonge/index.html

[103] Elad Filler, & Translated by Michael Carasik. (2016). Philo's Threefold Divine Vision and the Christian Trinity. *Hebrew Union College Annual, 87,* 93–113. https://doi.org/10.15650/hebruniocollannu.87.2016.0093

[104] David Runia, *Philo of Alexandria: An Annotated Bibliography,* (Radice and Runia, 2000: 136).

---

3.   https://www.scientificamerican.com/article/quantum-slits-open-new-doors/#_853ae90f0351324bd73ea615e6487517__4c761f170e016836ff84498202b99827__853ae90f0351324bd73ea615e6487517_text_43ec3e5dee6e706af7766fffea512721_In_0bcef9c45bd8a48eda1b26eb0c61c869_20the_0bcef9c45bd8a48eda1b26eb0c61c869_20experiment_0bcef9c45bd8a48eda1b26eb0c61c869_2C_0bcef9c45bd8a48eda1b26eb0c61c869_20first_0bcef9c45bd8a48eda1b26eb0c61c869_20proposed_0bcef9c45bd8a48eda1b26eb0c61c869_20in_0bcef9c45bd8a48eda1b26eb0c61c869_201801_0bcef9c45bd8a48eda1b26eb0c61c869_20by_c0cb5f0fcf239ab3d9c1fcd31fff1efc_a_0bcef9c45bd8a48eda1b26eb0c61c869_20wall_0bcef9c45bd8a48eda1b26eb0c61c869_20with_0bcef9c45bd8a48eda1b26eb0c61c869_20two_0bcef9c45bd8a48eda1b26eb0c61c869_20slits_0bcef9c45bd8a48eda1b26eb0c61c869_20cut_0bcef9c45bd8a48eda1b26eb0c61c869_20in_0bcef9c45bd8a48eda1b26eb0c61c869_20it.

[105] Novatian, *The Trinity, The Spectacles, Jewish Foods, In Praise of Purity, Letters*, ed. Hermigild Dressler, trans. Russell J. DeSimone, vol. 67, The Fathers of the Church (Washington, DC: The Catholic University of America Press, 1974), iii.

[106] James Hastings, John A. Selbie, and John C. Lambert, eds., "Christ," *A Dictionary of Christ and the Gospels: Aaron–Zion* (Edinburgh; New York: T&T Clark; Charles Scribner's Sons, 1906), 876.

[107] Ibid, p. 878.

[108] Ibid. pp. 877-891.

[109] Ibid, p. 878.

[110] Josephus's *Against Apion*, 2. 190–219.

[111] Pieter W. van der Horst, "Jewish Literature: Historians and Poets," *Dictionary of New Testament Background: A Compendium of Contemporary Biblical Scholarship* (Downers Grove, IL: InterVarsity Press, 2000), 582–583.

[112] Arthur G. Patzia and Anthony J. Petrotta, *Pocket Dictionary of Biblical Studies* (Downers Grove, IL: InterVarsity Press, 2002), 117.

[113] Jacob Neusner, "Rabbinic Literature: Mishnah and Tosefta," *Dictionary of New Testament Background: A Compendium of Contemporary Biblical Scholarship* (Downers Grove, IL: InterVarsity Press, 2000), 895.

[114] Genesis Rabbah 1:2, 6th Century. I, Dr. Jeffrey Johnson, *God Was There, Genesis Chapters 1-12*, (Wipf and Stock Publishers, Eugene, OR.). pp.1,2., 2005.

[115] Mishneh Torah, *Yesodey ha-Torah* 1:6.